ANT

ONCE UPON A TYNE

&

OUR STORY CELEBRATING 30 YEARS TOGETHER ON TELLY

DEC

with Andy Milligan

To the fans, old and new, that
continue to watch and support us.

- Chapter 3 -

CONTENTS

- Chapter 5 -

- Chapter 6 -

- Chapter 7 -

- Chapter 8 -

- Chapter 10 -

PROLOGUE

Thirty years ago, the world was a very different place.

Margaret Thatcher was the Prime Minister.

Vanilla Ice was topping the charts.

And, in the biggest shock of all, Ant hadn't met Dec.

But that was all about to change . . .

We'll get to the details of the earth-shattering event when one smaller-than-average 14-year-old Geordie met another shortly, but before we go any further, we should quickly explain that when you see words in bold, that's me, Dec – because, as a person, I'm quite bold.

And when you see words in italics, that's me, Ant – because as a person, I often stand at a jaunty angle.

What?

That doesn't really work, does it? Just remember, Ant – italics . . .

. . . and Dec – bold. OK?

Great.

Right, let's get on to the important stuff – this book. So why are we writing it? Well, quite simply, 30 years ago, I met a very special person.

Wow, who was that?

You. I thought you felt the same?

I did.

'Did'?

Do. Still do.

Thank you. This year is the 30th anniversary of when we met and started working together (that's why we began by talking about Margaret Thatcher and Vanilla Ice) and, to celebrate that, we wanted to tell you the story of the last three decades, with all the behind-the-scenes tales and ridiculous moments from 30 years of Ant and Dec.

Sometimes it feels like those three decades have gone by in the blink of an eye and sometimes it feels like it's been 100 years since we met. In a nice way. But the important thing is that we've been by each other's side the whole time – from paintballing accidents and being in a constant state of readiness for any rhumbling that may be required, to me chatting up Mariah Carey at a wedding . . .

It was in a sketch on *sm:tv*, in case you thought you'd missed a big showbiz scoop.

. . . to feeding Caitlyn Jenner a cow's eyeball, and finally hitting number one in the singles chart. And this book follows the story of all that. It's what one might call a 'professional memoir'.

If one was feeling very pretentious?

Indeed.
  And there are so many other reasons we wanted to write this book; we're proud of staying together for 30 years and proud of making us work for three decades. We also wanted

a record of our career, partly because our memories are getting worse as we get older.

They are not.
   Right, what are we doing again?

A book.

Oh yeah, sorry.
   What's it about?

Two blokes off the telly, Ant and thingy.
   As I was saying, we're writing the book partly so we don't forget things and partly so that our families can have something to read in the future, when they don't believe we actually did any of this stuff.

We already have enough trouble getting them to believe half the things we've done. To this day, my nephews think I'm making up the fact that Alan Shearer once woke me up with a cup of tea in bed (that's a little teaser for the main tea-based story in the book . . .).
   And, talking of famous people, we also wanted to chart some of the other relationships we've had in the last three decades, with those people who've been a huge part of our story – like one of our first comedy writers, David Walliams, and the people who've had cameos in our double act, like Cat Deeley and Stephen Mulhern, plus recurring characters like Robbie Williams and Simon Cowell.
   And we'll be hearing from them throughout the book – if they're nice about us, they might even get their own font.

In their own different ways, those people have all played a role in us two being on your telly screens for so long.

Why else do you think people have let us stick around all this time, Ant?

Hmm, good question – thanks, Dec. I hope in part it's because people see themselves reflected in us. I mean, who doesn't love trying to make their best mate laugh? That's basically all we've ever done.

And when it comes to our double act, we've tried not to have any individual ego, haven't we? We've always felt that if Ant OR Dec was getting a laugh, we were both getting a laugh. Sometimes, one of us will be the butt of the joke about, say, let me think . . .

You being smaller than the average human man? Just as an example off the top of my head.

Good one. But don't you mean, 'off the top of my abnormally large forehead'?
   The point is, if people are laughing at one of us, it's a laugh we share.

You know what else worked out well? When it comes to our partnership off screen, I think we have different strengths.

Definitely. Ant is unpredictable and ready to push the boundaries, and he's also brilliant at taking an idea, building on it and making me laugh.

And Dec's the same, he makes me laugh harder than anyone else in the world. He also knows our audience inside out and how to give them exactly what they want, which sometimes is a joke about the fact he's only five foot six.

Five foot six and a half. Not that it's a big deal.

I think we also share a passion for perfection. Whatever we do, we work as hard as we can to make it the very best it can be. That's something we've always had in common.

But at the heart of.it all is our friendship, we're nothing without that. Which is why, in a lot of ways, this book is a love story. Because we really do care deeply about each other and, ultimately, we love each other. And a big part of that, especially these days, now that we're older and we've been through more life experiences, is that we check in on each other much more, we keep an eye on how we're each doing.

Our priorities have changed since we started out; our lives are very different from how they were in the nineties and noughties when we were young men—

You mean, 'when we were young__er__ men'.

But the funny thing is, that change in priorities has made us enjoy and value work all the more. We're incredibly lucky to do what we do, and we've never lost sight of that.

So that's who we are, where we're at and why we wanted to write this book. And before you ask, yes, there will be photos. Lots of photos. Although let's be honest, if you've got this book in your hand, you've already looked at the photos, haven't you? You probably had a look in the shop. Some of you probably just had a look at the photos in the shop and then didn't even buy the book . . . but then you won't be reading this bit.

We're getting sidetracked.

As well as photos, there will be funny stories about showbusiness – each chapter covers a different TV show or piece of work we've starred in, from *Byker Grove* in 1990 right up to the 2020 series of *Saturday Night Takeaway*. So, what do you reckon, shall we get cracking?

If you ask me, there's only one thing to say: Let's get ready toooo . . .

Start the book about our 30 years together?

Not quite how I was going to put it, but it'll do.

1

BYKER GROVE

Shall we start by telling the lovely reader about that magical day we met for the very first time?

Definitely.

Do you remember it?

Not especially. You?

Bits. But let's have a go at piecing it together, shall we?

Yes – and like all the greatest stories, it begins with an everyday tale of a youth club in Newcastle that was televised every Wednesday and Friday at ten past five on CBBC straight after *Newsround*.

**   *Byker Grove* was a drama aimed at young adults and teenagers. The characters faced issues like teenage pregnancy or drug addiction alongside lighter, more comic capers. It ran from 1989 to 2006 and launched the careers of Anthony McPartlin and Declan Donnelly.**

Did you get that from Wikipedia?

Whatever gave you that idea?

**   In 1989, a year before Ant arrived, I'd been cast in *Byker Grove* and was already firmly ensconced in the part of 'Duncan', a young man who looked and sounded a lot like 13-year-old Declan Donnelly. His main narrative arcs in the first season included standing in the background of a youth club disco and standing in the background of a youth club game of table tennis.**

Daylight robbery you didn't get a BAFTA.

In the first season—

'Season'? It's not Game of Thrones.

In the first series, which only had six episodes, I/Duncan mainly spent time with the younger members of the cast, other teenagers from Newcastle who frequented the youth club, like Lyndyann Barrass, who played Spuggie, John Jefferson, who played Spuggie's brother Fraser, and Craig Reilly, who took the role of Winston.

Being such a short series, the whole thing was filmed in about six weeks, which meant I didn't make loads of friends until series 2, which had a whopping 20 episodes. But in that second series, there was definitely still a bond between the Original Grovers, or the OGs, as we'd have been called if we were gangster rappers. Which we definitely weren't.

Shall we just get to the bit where I turn up?

Well, I think we just need a bit more background on my sterling thespian work as Duncan first. I think my finest scene was . . .

Right, I'll do it then.

It was series 2 when I was cast as PJ. Also the series where the number of episodes jumped from six to 20. Coincidence?

I would've thought so.

You're probably right.

And I still remember turning up for my first day, taking a deep breath and heading into The Mitre, which was an old pub that doubled as the youth club set in Byker Grove.

To give you an idea of how significant that place was for us, 21 years later, when we set up our TV production company, we called it Mitre.

– Ant's singing voice was 'appreciated'
from an early age. –

– What do you call a man with a cabbage on his head?
Dec, evidently. –

As I walked into The Mitre, I was, how shall I put this? Bricking it. As a new cast member, it was like walking in halfway through a party where you didn't know anyone. The Original Grovers all had their own in-jokes and running gags and I felt like a real outsider. Even though the producers and the chaperones tried to get me involved, it was tough. Not least because on the first day, we were exposed to the worst three words in the English language: improvisational theatre games.

I don't remember any of this.

That's because you already felt at home.
   As if that wasn't bad enough, keep in mind that at this point I was a 14-year-old boy, with all the insecurities and awkwardness that brought. I had a terrible haircut, with a big cowlick at the front and, after some recent dental work, funny-looking teeth with temporary crowns. As a kid, I suffered with brittle enamel thanks to being born two months premature and, throughout my childhood, I was self-conscious about my teeth.
   None of this did wonders for my confidence. All in all, I just remember focusing on keeping my head down and feeling absolutely terrified.

You're breaking my heart here; I had no idea.

On the plus side (not that I knew it then), that was the last time I'd ever have to go through anything like that alone. After Byker Grove, every time I met people for the first time, every time I went somewhere new and strange, every time I had to negotiate a weird situation, I was with Dec and we were in it together.

We certainly were.

Now, shall we stop holding hands and get back to that first day?

PJ, who was a DJ, was rebellious and cool . . . or as rebellious and cool as anyone who wore an oversized baseball cap and had a name that rhymed with his hobby could be.

Me and Ant didn't make much of an impression on each other at first, but we did have one thing in common: a fascination with television, even if for most of our childhoods, we had no idea it was an option as a career.

The start of it for me was loving drama at school. It just felt different, more exciting than any other subject I did, and a huge part of that was my secondary school drama teacher, Lyn Spencer. She was so encouraging, and drama became a class where I could be myself, and also where I was treated more like an adult.

Then one day, the producers of Byker Grove came to our school and asked if anybody wanted to come to an audition. And Lyn put me forward. Without that, I never would have done it – getting that kind of encouragement at an early age is so, so important.

For me, encouragement came from a different source – the Tyneside Irish Centre. My parents started running it before I was born and stayed at the helm for the first ten years of my life. I spent a lot of time there as a kid and was always fascinated by the bands or performers that came in to do the live entertainment. They were the centre of attention for the evening and their job was to make sure everyone had a great Saturday night.

Sounds familiar . . .

The other thing that made an impact on me was a local drama group. During the summer holidays from school, I went to something at our local community centre called 'Cruddas MAD'. Cruddas Park is the area of Newcastle I grew up in and MAD stood for Music and Drama.

In all our 30 years, I've never heard you talk about Cruddas MAD.

Nice to know I can still surprise you.

I went there with my sisters Moyra and Camalia over the summer holidays and, as well as providing us kids from the estate with something to do, Cruddas MAD sparked something in me: a love of performing.

But back to the Grove, and as well as the kids we've mentioned, there were also actual grown adults involved, including 'Little' Billy Fane, who played Geoff, the youth leader who ran the place. As a well-known performer in the Northeast and an experienced actor, Billy was someone we all admired. And then there was the producer, Matthew Robinson, he was very much the captain of the good ship *Byker Grove*.

Matthew's a crucial person in our story – he was the one who gave us our big Byker Grove *break. He taught us how important it was to be professional. He made us understand the importance of turning up on time, knowing our lines and being respectful to the crew.*

Shame he forgot to teach us how to act, but you can't have everything, can you?

For the first series we both appeared in, we didn't have loads of storylines or scenes together, but the turning point came when PJ set up a pirate radio station in the attic of the Grove and Duncan got involved. The more scenes PJ and Duncan had together, the more scenes Ant and Dec had together – largely because PJ was Ant and Duncan was Dec, in case you missed that key piece of information.

But the biggest moment of our burgeoning bromance—

Excellent use of 'burgeoning'.

Thanks.
. . . was when Ant sent me a Fred Flintstone Christmas card asking me if I wanted to go and watch Newcastle United play Swindon Town on Boxing Day.

I didn't send a Christmas card to all my mates that year, it wasn't the kind of thing I normally did – but my mam had one card left in the multipack and when I saw the message on the front saying, 'Have A Yabba Dabba Doo Christmas!', I thought, 'That'll make Dec laugh.'

And it did.
So, on Boxing Day 1990, we met up for the first time away from *Byker Grove.* **We spent the first part of it looking round the clothes shops in High Bridge, where we lusted after various desirable items of the day: baggy jeans, Caterpillar boots, Fila trainers and hoodies. And then we had a pasty from Greggs and went to the match, in what surely qualifies as 'most Geordie way to spend an afternoon ever'. After that, we were officially friends . . . not that we said as much to each other at the time.**

Initially, we became good mates because we had so much in common. A lot of our friendship back then revolved around three things: football, telly and music. We both absolutely loved Vic Reeves Big Night Out *on Channel 4 and spent half*

2006. Returning to the scene of our first date. –

– Dec loved the camera so much you couldn't get him to put it down. –

The best damn twice-weekly-Newcastle-based-kids-drama football team ever. –

– The *Byker Grove* Human Pyramid Display Team didn't get much work. –

our lives saying, 'You wouldn't let it lie' to each other, often over the phone. Back then our phone was in the front room, so I would stretch the cord out and sit behind the sofa. Me and Dec would swap Vic and Bob (Mortimer) catchphrases for hours on end, all while the rest of the family took turns trying to watch the TV and telling me to shut up.

It was before the internet. There was literally nothing else to do.

I remember a cinema trip where we went to see *Wayne's World* together and that just blew our minds. We couldn't believe a film could be that funny, not to mention packed with a brand-new set of catchphrases for us to relentlessly repeat to each other.

And of course, with the benefit of hindsight, it seems significant that, just like Vic and Bob, Wayne and Garth were a double act.

Our other shared love – music – mainly involved reading the *NME*, and we loved indie bands from Manchester like the Happy Mondays and Inspiral Carpets. That was the first gig we went to together, Inspiral Carpets, at the Newcastle Mayfair. We'd both dutifully bought their album two weeks earlier from HMV on Northumberland Street and learnt every word, ready to sing along at the gig. We had the time of our lives that night, surrounded by fellow baggy-clothed indie fans.

Still one of my favourite ever gigs. Over the next year or so, we became inseparable – and, as well as gigs, we went to plenty of football matches together. Although that wasn't always a pleasant experience – and not just because of how bad Newcastle United were back then. When we got recognised by lads our own age in town, they'd often follow us, threaten to chin us and then mix those threats up with a lovely bit of spitting at us. All because we were 'them kids off Byker Grove'.

Not the best reviews we've ever had . . .

That kind of stuff carried on the whole time we were in the show, not constantly but enough to make us avoid places other kids our age went to. Once we were old enough to go to the pub, you'd often find us off the beaten track, in student bars, that sort of thing. We'd never go to the Bigg Market, the epicentre of any night out in 1990s Newcastle, because we wanted to avoid being recognised and picked on. It meant we felt a bit different from most other kids our age.

But most of the time, when we weren't getting spat at, it was a good kind of different. And we had each other – someone else going through exactly the same thing – which made it a hell of a lot easier.

And we always felt at home at work.

That sounded confusing.

We always felt comfortable at work, that's what I mean. And as our time on *Byker Grove* went on, we became more and more captivated by how television was made.

And with no Google, you had to just ask people, so we'd be forever quizzing the camera and lighting team about why they set up shots the way they did and why they used certain lenses or tripods. And they indulged us, they answered our questions and we learnt so much – and, what's more, we learnt it at work, on an actual set, rather than from a book, and that was incredibly valuable.

Sometimes, we even learnt from each other. I remember

seeing one of Dec's scripts and he'd marked up all his lines in the scene with a highlighter pen.

Not because I thought they'd be the highlight of the scene, but because it made them easier to pick out and learn – I'm sure most actors do it, but I wasn't 'most actors', I was a '14-year-old kid who lived with his mam and dad'.

I'd also make a note in my script of where I'd come from in my previous scene and what Duncan's mood was, so that I could keep it consistent – you don't want to leave one scene in tears and then turn up in your next scene laughing your head off; you'd look weird.

I was impressed. I remember thinking, 'This kid's got it.'

And by 'it', he meant a 99p highlighter pen from WHSmith.

But we still do that now: if we're shooting something like Men in Brown *(our comedy drama sketch for* Saturday Night Takeaway *2020), we'll both still highlight our scripts.*

Not with the same highlighter pen. Tragically, it ran out of day-glo pink ink in 1992 after a good innings, but the principle is the same.

And in terms of what was actually in those beautifully highlighted scripts, well, let's just say PJ and Duncan got themselves into all sorts of scrapes.

Like Duncan getting mixed up in a cult. A cult called, wait for it, Psychandrics.
    Duncan was brainwashed, you see, although anyone who joins a cult called Psychandrics in early nineties Newcastle doesn't have that much of a brain to wash, if you ask me. But they got to him via a girl he fancied. And

Duncan fell for the whole thing hook, line and sinker. It all culminated in Duncan standing in the middle of Newcastle city centre (at Grey's Monument if you're interested, fact fans) dressed in what looked suspiciously like a pair of pyjamas.

The other characters tried to get Duncan to snap out of it, shouting stuff like, 'Wake up, Duncan!', which was actually a perfectly sensible thing to say to someone dressed in pyjamas.

To make matters worse, filming in the centre of Newcastle usually meant you'd bump into someone you knew. I just prayed (to the cult leader of Psychandrics, obviously) that I didn't see any of my mates. But those prayers fell on deaf ears and one of my best friends was in town that day – and he spent the whole time laughing his head off at me.

Yeah, sorry about that, it was just so funny.

I also saw one of my mam's friends and we enjoyed the following exchange:

'Are you Fonsey and Anne's littl'un?'
'Yes.'
'Are you still in that TV show?'

(I resisted the temptation to respond with, 'No, I'm actually in the middle of a particularly intense bout of sleepwalking' and went with the following . . .)

'Yes, I'm filming it right now.'
'Is that why you're wearing them pyjamas?'
'Yes.'
'Well, tell your mam I said hello.'
'Will do.'
'Bye.'

Much as I enjoyed laughing at Duncan in pjs, I had my own nightmares with filming too, although mine were more self-inflicted. Towards the end of our time on the Grove, I went to a mate from school's 18th and the next morning woke up with a hangover that can only be described as 'absolutely bloody horrendous'. I remember lying in bed, thinking, 'When was the last time anyone felt this bad wearing a pair of pyjamas?'

I think I can probably answer that . . .

I knew I was filming for Byker Grove that day, but I was hoping it would be a nice quiet shoot where I could keep my head down and get through the day. And then I remembered one crucial detail about the storyline we were doing. We were filming at the Junior Great North Run. And we were going to be dressed as Teenage Mutant Ninja Turtles.

It made joining Psychandrics look like a walk in the park.

Down the years I've heard lots of different suggestions about the best way to cure a hangover, but I have never, ever heard anyone say, 'If you want to feel better, make sure you immediately do the Junior Great North Run dressed as a Teenage Mutant Ninja Turtle.'

I thought about trying to get out of it, or just jumping in a hedge and hiding for a couple of weeks, but I was a professional (sort of), so I had to just suck it up and get on with the day.

I'm so glad I was there for this.

So you could support me and offer a shoulder to cry on?

No, so I could laugh at you. It was hilarious.

On the off-chance you haven't committed that full episode to memory, we were dressed as turtles because PJ and Duncan were doing the run in fancy dress for charity. And the outfits were awful, not because the wardrobe department were rubbish – they were brilliant (after all, they'd created a whole 'look' that revolved around baseball caps for PJ . . .) – but because our turtle costumes were meant to look homemade. So we ended up running around in white boiler suits made out of paper and painted green, with homemade shells on our backs and turtle masks from a joke shop.

I told Ant he should lighten up and 'come out of his shell a bit'.

I would have punched him, but I was far too busy focusing on not throwing up all over my boiler suit.

Strangely, it just seemed to make things worse when I told him he looked 'turtle-y awful'. Incidentally, if you're not from Newcastle and you want to do a good Geordie accent, replace the word 'totally' with the word 'turtle-y'. It works perfectly.
    You're trying it now, aren't you? You're welcome.

It was arguably the worst day at work I've ever had. But I got through it. Just.

With a little help from me, of course.

Interesting use of the word 'help'.
    But the fact that we enjoyed each other's on-set misfortunes so much was another sign that, slowly but surely, we were becoming a bit of a double act. They used to have posters of all the cast members in the production office, so that when fans wrote in (yes, it happened, get over it) the office would send them back a signed poster of their favourite character.

There was one of me and Dec – it's been used on pretty much every chat show we've ever been guests on.

And there's a good reason for that – it's hilarious. I've got a classic nineties 'curtains' hairstyle and Ant's in a red cap and a waistcoat, but you try looking at pictures of yourself from the early nineties and not cringing, eh?

Anyway, this poster – it was the first time they'd done anything in publicity terms that was just the two of us together. We would never have called ourselves a double act back then, but these posters were very popular and I just remember me and Dec sitting in the production offices, signing poster after poster after poster and, looking back, it was the first acknowledgement from the public that they liked us a pair.

And our most significant storyline as a pair started with a sentence that has followed us two around for almost 30 years.

No, not 'Which one's Ant and which one's Dec?' It's this:

'He cannot see, can he? He can't see, man!'

PJ getting blinded in a horrific paintballing accident was one of our last storylines and it made a big impact, especially on one young girl in the West Midlands.

CAT DEELEY: *'Like every other teenage girl, I was devastated when PJ had his accident and became blind.'*

Poor teenage Cat, thanks for the feedback Ms Deeley (much more from her later).

– Grove Matrix's debut gig.
Background: Sparkly curtains.
Foreground Dec's curtains. –

– Grove Matrix and the 1992
winner of 'Newcastle's
Longest Keyboard'. –

– Dec and Ant the wrong way round! (Anything to
avoid talking about the outfits . . .) –

It was a storyline we did quite a lot of research for. *Byker Grove* tackled its fair share of 'issues' back in the day, from teenage pregnancy to bullying, and as part of that research, we both went to a blind school in Newcastle, spent some time with kids there who had lost their sight and spoke to them about their experiences.

We also worked with a mobility officer who taught me how to use a cane and showed Dec how you would guide a blind person. She even got me to cross a busy road in Newcastle with a blindfold on. The whole experience was a real education; we were only 17 at the time and we'd never had to think about living with disability, as I'm sure a lot of the audience hadn't. It was a huge privilege for us both to be involved in such a significant storyline.

Series 5 of *Byker Grove* (criminally still overlooked by Netflix when it's so bingeworthy) was dominated by PJ's blindness and, with PJ and Duncan as two of the main characters, the story took a turn the audience weren't expecting – they formed a boy band called Grove Matrix. Much like the Rolling Stones, Oasis or Five, Grove Matrix had five members, but the similarities ended there.
Along with PJ and Duncan, the line-up was completed by those other Grove stalwarts Barney, Marcus and Frew.

As part of the storyline, we were sent to record a proper actual track called 'Tonight I'm Free'. Part of me wanted to make the full title 'Tonight I'm Free (From A Hangover And That Bloody Ninja Turtle Costume)' but no one else was having any of it. The song was featured in an episode of the show where Grove Matrix did their first gig, which went down a storm, thanks largely to a room full of paid extras who were told, 'Make it look like this is going down a storm.'

This storyline really took PJ and Duncan to the next level – they had their own song, they were the main characters, and even more fan mail started to arrive at the *Byker Grove* offices for us. The big question was: could things get any better?

And the big answer was: 'No. Actually, they're about to get quite a lot worse.' We got called into our producer Matthew's office for a chat. He told us we'd done a great job and that our characters had been a huge hit.

Looking back, his use of the past tense should have been a giveaway . . .

But there was a problem, one that had started to worry some of the bosses at CBBC – and, incredibly, it wasn't our vocals on 'Tonight I'm Free'. They thought the audience for Byker Grove was getting too old – and the job of the show was to attract younger viewers. To do that, they needed younger characters.

The penny still hadn't dropped. Partly because I'd switched off at the words, 'Your characters have been a huge hit.' In the end, Matthew had to spell it out for us: PJ and Duncan were just too old to be hanging out at a youth club so they wouldn't be coming back, they were leaving the Grove for good, this was the end, our time on the show was over.

It was a masterclass in saying, 'You're sacked' without ever saying, 'You're sacked.'

And, to be fair to Matthew, he found it hard and you could tell he really felt for us. He'd even pitched the BBC a PJ and Duncan spin-off show, but they weren't interested.

It still remains one of the most difficult moments of our career – we were both doing what we loved with our best mate and, in the blink of an eye, it was all taken away from us. After a handshake from Matthew, who thanked us for taking the news so well, we left, absolutely shell-shocked – and with no idea what was coming next.

We were in real danger of being on the scrapheap at 18; it felt like our whole world had fallen in. And then, something incredible happened.

Matthew burst out of his office and shouted, 'Stop! Stop! Stop! Telstar Records have just been on the phone, and they want to offer you a record contract.'

We couldn't believe it; the timing was worthy of the most incredible TV drama. But us two? Become pop stars? We thought it was a practical joke.

That moment changed our lives for ever. It led us to our pop career, which led to us making kids' TV shows, which led us to Saturday night telly, all of which led us to 30 years together and this book.

But we're getting ahead of ourselves. We had a pop career to get on with, which means it's time to tell you about every single one of the huge musical successes we enjoyed.

And when we've finished that page, we'll tell you about the rest of it.

The *Byker Grove* cast with their version of the Sgt Pepper album cover. –

– Returning in 2006 to The
Mitre, which is Latin for
'Massive Blue Door'. –

– 2012, *Byker Grove* cast reunion: 'You
haven't changed a bit . . . height-wise.' –

2

THE POP
STAR YEARS

TEN THINGS THAT HAPPENED TO PJ & DUNCAN THE MOST:

1. Being spat on by fans' boyfriends.
2. Miming (badly) to a backing track on teen TV shows.
3. Running competitions to 'Have lunch with PJ & Duncan'.
    (Second prize: Two lunches with PJ & Duncan.)
4. Sharing a room at Travelodges while on tour.
5. Eating Ginsters pasties from service stations on tour.
6. Travelling abroad without appreciating any of it (mainly
    thanks to a lack of Ginsters pasties).
7. Being sent teddy bears by fans (7,521 to be exact).
8. Performing 'Let's Get Ready To Rhumble'.
9. Having to spell the word rumble wrong.
10. Never really feeling at home being pop stars.

*That list, along with the extensive collection of embarrassing
photos you've already laughed at at least twice, pretty much
sums up our life as pop stars, although honourable mentions
should also go to other great moments: Dec posing topless, me
shaving my head and Dec accidentally dyeing his hair ginger.*

Those highlights really were lowlights.

But, as you'll remember from four whole pages ago, it
all started out with a record deal from Telstar to release
'Tonight I'm Free'. And that deal spoke volumes about
the faith the record label had in us, because they made
a commitment – no matter what happened, they would
release, get ready for it, one whole single. I know,
incredible, right?

- Ant: 'I'm sure this is how
Spiderman does it.' Dec: 'Your hand
needs to be the other way up, mate.'
-

Dec's preferred mode of transport. -

- So glad we both still have a set of that bedding; the
thread count is superb. -

At the beginning, we were worried about becoming the kind of cheesy TV spin-off pop stars we'd always laughed at. But even though we were a couple of indie kids at heart, there was one thing that made all those worries instantly evaporate. We were unemployed actors with no job prospects who lived at home with our mams. Funny how that kind of thing can stop you worrying about the creative direction of your fledgling pop career . . .

Telstar told us the response to Grove Matrix on *Byker Grove* had been huge and viewers had written in asking where they could buy the single. And yes, with sentences like 'viewers had written in', I am aware that it sounds like this all happened in 1962, but it was a time when there was no iTunes, no Spotify and the music industry was a very different place. The record label said we had a ready-made fanbase and, even though we knew deep down we were never really going to be the next Take That, we put on a pair of baggy jeans and went for it.

A pair of baggy jeans each, that is. We didn't share the same pair. Although with the size of jeans in the early nineties, you could have housed a family of six inside each trouser leg.

And that was it, we launched Operation: Pop Career.

We're calling it an operation because it was very painful, and it took a long time to recover from. In total, it lasted four years and rather than go into every last detail of those four years, we're going to do something we never managed in our music career.

Deliver the greatest hits – the best, the worst and the weirdest bits from the life and times of PJ & Duncan.

And we start on a train from Newcastle to Birmingham in late 1993, when we were 18 years old and on our way to our first-ever gig, the TV Hits Roadshow. The funny thing about that journey is that, in some ways, it was the day we left home, but in lots of other ways, we still haven't officially left home.

What Ant means is that although neither of us has really lived in Newcastle full-time since that day, we never had that big farewell moment where we said goodbye to our families and our lives in Newcastle. We went back after the TV Hits Roadshow, but we instantly got into a cycle of three or four weeks in London – staying at a hotel and making an appearance in the CBBC broom cupboard (fun) or doing a *My Guy* magazine photoshoot (cringey) – followed by a couple of days back home where we'd briefly see our family and get our washing done.

Thank you to our mams.
Not just for washing – they are both amazing mams.
I remember that on those trips to London, we were told to always keep our train tickets and our receipts for food and send them to the record label in an envelope, so they could send us a cheque for our expenses.

Oh, the glamour . . .
The gaps between our trips back to our houses in Newcastle got longer and longer and, 30 years later, I suppose it's time to finally admit we've left home.

We're just sorry our mams had to find out like this.

In the beginning, we'd perform at a lot of after-school discos and one of the by-products of that was that girls would start screaming at us.

The first time it happened, it was weird and then after that, well, we bloody loved it. After all, if you're going to be a pop star then it comes with the territory. Unfortunately, what also came with the territory at those after-school discos was the girls' boyfriends spitting at us and even throwing the odd ice cube or ashtray.

But despite the identified flying objects, we did have a few high points, and we couldn't do the PJ & Duncan chapter without mentioning the finest track of our pop career. I am of course talking about . . .

'Boom There She Was'. Track 14 on the Japanese deluxe version of our second album, but then you already know that. And it went a little something like this . . .

I was talking about 'Let's Get Ready To Rhumble'.

Oh yeah, that one.

It was our third single and one of our many deliberately misspelt classics (others included 'U Krazy Katz' and 'Top Katz'). Right from the off, 'Rhumble' — and, yes, that's what I'm calling it from now on — felt like a classic pop tune. We even got to perform it on *Live and Kicking*, a BBC1 Saturday morning kids' show hosted by Andi Peters. Hi Andi! (He'll definitely read this book to see if he's in it.)

Bye Andi! (He definitely won't read on now he's seen his mention.) 'Rhumble' went on to peak at number nine in July 1994, which was a huge deal for us. Even more importantly, it was the track that secured our first appearance on Top of the Pops. Like everyone our age, we grew up watching that show and to appear on it was a dream come true.

At the time, there was a lot of talk about whether acts should sing live or not. A lot of pop acts – including us – mimed to a backing track for many of their performances, but we took the decision to sing—

Or, more accurately, 'talk fast'.

. . . live. And I don't mind telling you, when it came to the big day, we were absolutely terrified, but we practised and practised and practised and we actually pulled it off. We talked fast, live, on *Top of the Pops* and didn't make fools of ourselves.

And for all you fact fans, number one that week was Wet Wet Wet's 'Love Is All Around' and, also appearing on the show were Clubhouse, Bad Boys Inc., The Grid, CJ Lewis and Skin. Incredibly, the show's host was the very funny Julian Clary.

Apart from actually performing on TOTP, one of the biggest thrills was going to the canteen. Not for their egg and chips—

Although they did a mean egg and chips.

– but because TOTP was filmed at BBC Elstree Studios, which was also where they made EastEnders. So, you'd be sat in the canteen, thinking, 'Oh my God, look over there. There's Michelle Fowler, there's Ethel and her little Willy, there's Wet Wet Wet sat next to Pete Beale.' EastEnders was one of the biggest shows on TV at the time and we were so starstruck – to us two, the Elstree canteen was like the Hollywood Walk of Fame.

As well as the bands we were on *Top of the Pops* with, we'd obviously see a lot of our contemporaries at the various roadshows and TV appearances. Take That and East 17 were the big guns at the time, and we'd usually appear alongside people like Ultimate Kaos, Sean Maguire, 911 and Michelle Gayle. On one tour, we were even supported by an American band called the Backstreet Boys; not sure what happened to them . . .

Compared to a lot of those acts and despite our success at 'live talking', we always had a degree of impostor syndrome when it came to our music career. We felt like we were playing the part of pop stars, rather than being actual pop stars. I think that helped us get through the whole experience without getting too carried away when things went well or too down in the dumps when things went badly.

The funny thing is that once people see you as a pop star, they automatically assume you have an impossibly glamorous life: that you live in a mansion with a swimming pool, a jacuzzi and a football pitch in the back garden. Spoiler alert: we didn't.

At first, during our trips to London, we'd share a double room in a Travelodge. It didn't have a bath, never mind a jacuzzi. Eventually, we graduated to a hotel in Chelsea called La Reserve, which is French for 'The Reserve'.

Dec's always had an aptitude for languages. Next stop after La Reserve was the Hilton in Olympia, which is memorable for two reasons. Firstly, they had a snack on the bar that we christened 'Curried Swirls' – and, in an attempt to save money, we would often eat bowls and bowls of them as our evening meal.

And, secondly, we were there so long that we put up posters on the wall of our room. Yes – we were so at home in the hotel, we made it into the average teenager's bedroom. I remember posters of Supergrass and one of Kylie Minogue adorning the walls of room 117.

Of course, we both missed home and our families, but in some ways, living together down in 'that London' made up for it – it felt very exciting and, most importantly of all, it was paid for by someone else.

Our next stop was the Marriott in Swiss Cottage.

Does the reader really want to hear about every hotel we've ever stayed in?

This is the last one – and I'm about to mention some famous people.

Fair enough.

The bar in the Marriott was always lively. One night Oasis were in after an appearance on *TOTP* and their guitarist Bonehead got the two of us in a (friendly) headlock and declared it was time to 'Get on it with a couple of Geordies'. I don't really remember much after that.

We also ran into Robbie Williams there one evening – he came in just after he'd left Take That.

ROBBIE WILLIAMS: 'I remember meeting "Peej and Deej" at the Marriott. The lads were sat in the corner, each drinking a pint and I thought, "Oh, they're just like me!"'

We had a few drinks and he asked us if we thought he'd made the right decision leaving Take That.

- Dec and Ant, the wron
way round again! (Anythi
to avoid talking about th
outfits again . . .) -

- A roadshow in Liverpool, 1994 -

- The aforementioned headlock with Bonehead. -

We told him he definitely had . . . because, well, what else were we going to say? History proved us right, though, I'm happy to admit.

That conversation with Robbie did make me wonder if I should leave PJ & Duncan, but I thought better of it.

Eventually, someone at the record company worked out that it would be more cost-effective to rent us a flat than pay for hotel rooms every night, so we moved into a place in Fulham and then, towards the end of the pop days, to one in Chelsea Harbour. But we'd like to make it clear, there was definitely no jacuzzi and no football pitch in the garden.

One of them had a decent dishwasher, but that was about it.

Of course, we were often away from London, including one trip that threw up an event that we have been – and will be – asked about in every single interview we've ever done: our first fight. And it happened in the most exotic location imaginable: a trip to Torremolinos in Spain for GMTV's *Fun in the Sun*, the live show hosted by Anthea Turner.

It was a special summer holiday version of the ITV breakfast show and, in 1995, we were promoting 'Stuck On U', the first single from our second album, Top Katz. We arrived in the middle of a baking-hot July day and immediately experienced something no teen pop act ever, ever experiences – a day off. Our tour manager, the fiery and enthusiastic Kim Glover, told us we had the day to ourselves before appearing on GMTV the following morning, so after approximately 1.6 seconds we decided where we were going to go – the pub.

The next thing we knew, it was ten o'clock at night and we were pie-eyed, tucking into a full English breakfast.

You can take the boys out of Newcastle, but you can't take Newcastle out of the boys . . .

At around 10.30, Kim reappeared and politely suggested that, with a very early start, we might want to go and get some sleep, an offer we politely declined.

Eventually, several hours later, we decided to call it a night, partly because the night itself had decided to call it a night and hand over to the day.

I stood up and told Ant and Kim I was going to bed, when Ant shot back with a classic response:

'Where are you going?'
   It's the kind of hilarious back-and-forth banter we've built a career on.

I repeated I was off to bed and started stumbling towards the lift.

I did the sensible thing and said, 'What the hell are you going to bed for?' But Dec didn't answer and just kept stumbling towards the lift. Something about that incensed me and I lost it. With Kim trailing in my wake, I made a beeline for Dec. I almost fell into some bushes on the way, but I wanted words with him.
   And those words were, 'Don't you dare walk away from me when I'm talking to you.'

I stopped dead in my tracks and started ranting at Ant. Who the hell did he think he was, talking to me like that? (My argument was slightly compromised by several spots of egg yolk on my chin, but it was a great comeback nonetheless.) I don't mind telling you, he was really pushing my buttons.

Then the lift arrived, and Dec started pushing some buttons of his own, specifically the one marked '6'. He was still ranting and when he finally stopped – I think it was around the third floor – I said, 'If you've quite finished, I'd like to have my say.' Before Dec could reply, I started to rant back at him, but just a couple of sentences in he employed a complex and cunning strategy that often shuts down even the liveliest debate.

I put my fingers in my ears and started going, 'La, la, la, la, la, can't hear you.'

That made my blood boil, so I responded the only way I knew how. I punched Dec in the chest.

It was a blow that took the wind out of my sails – and my fingers out of my ears, but I quickly rallied and tried to knock Ant's cap off.

Obviously, I was wearing a cap. I was always wearing a cap.

Unfortunately, I didn't quite hit the target and ended up just punching the peak of his cap. I taught that cap a lesson that night, I can tell you. And the lesson was: 'Dec is rubbish at fighting when he's had a few.' And then Kim intervened, telling us to break it up – that's when both of us knew it wouldn't go any further. There were a few more 'verbals', but, basically, our aggression had hit its peak.

Much like Dec did with my cap.

The lift eventually arrived at our floor and we retreated back to our rooms, both feeling a combination of embarrassment and confusion about what had just happened.

The next morning, or about two hours later, to be more accurate, we put on our oversized day-glo shirts and headed for GMTV's Fun in the Sun. When I arrived, Dec was already there and there was only one thought in my head – make up.

Aw, I didn't know you wanted to apologise; that's lovely.

No, make-up, I needed to have make-up put on my face to get ready for the TV show.

Oh, right.

We both sat there in our respective chairs, having our make-up done but still maintaining our huffs from the night before. That's how people in light entertainment roll. 'I'm not even looking at you . . . because I'm busy watching a woman called Linda cover my face in foundation and gel my spiky hair within an inch of its life.'

Then we made our way to the set, with our hangovers getting worse by the second. This TV show might have been in the sun, but it was certainly not fun. But somewhere, somehow, through a haze of Heineken fumes, hair gel and lingering resentment, we put our partnership back together.

I remember turning to Dec just before the opening bars of 'Stuck On U' began and saying, 'Thank God we're still pissed.' He laughed, the ice was broken, and PJ & Duncan were reunited. By the time the performance had finished, it was like nothing had ever happened.

So that's the 'Epic Battle of Torremolinos', as literally no one has ever called it, but once we'd got over our first big tiff, we got back to doing what we did best – making absolute tits of ourselves in the name of pop success.

One guaranteed way of making someone who isn't 100 per cent committed to life as a pop star cringe is to make them do photoshoots.

We do them today for our TV shows, but what we know now that we didn't know then is that – and get ready for this revelation – you can say no to stuff the photographer suggests. Seems pretty obvious, right? Well, not to pop star Ant and pop star Dec. We were young and we didn't know any better and, before we knew it, we were being dressed up in Japanese kimonos, or being asked to 'show a bit more chest' by unbuttoning a shirt.

There are definitely pictures out there that we look at and think, 'I wish I'd said no to that', and those are the pictures from—

Our entire pop career?

Pretty much.

None of the pictures from those days really reflected who we were. We were listening to Blur and Oasis, but all the photoshoots portrayed us as ker-azy pop guys who wore oversized ice hockey tops.

And the same applied to interviews. These days, when we talk about TV, we can speak with a passion and a knowledge on the subject, but when someone asked us in 1995, 'What was the inspiration for your second album?' the only answer we had was,
'It meant we didn't have to move home and live with our mams.'
But you couldn't really say that to a journalist.

One of the other parts of Operation: Pop Career we struggled with was songwriting. Most of our first album was produced by a guy called Nicky Graham (who'd penned the Byker Grove anthem 'Tonight I'm Free') along with his songwriting team of Deni Lew and Mike Olton, but for the second album we got more involved in songwriting.

And immediately after that, in a shock twist, our record sales plummeted.

Weird, eh?
    For that second album, the record label put us with a few different writers (including a guy called Ray 'Madman' Hedges, who wrote most of it) and they'd encourage us but, basically, we didn't have a clue. We couldn't play any instruments and we'd spend interminably long days in the studio trying to come up with lyrics. It was excruciating.

Making videos, on the other hand, was always fun – being on a set took us back to *Byker Grove* days and an environment where we felt at home. Although videos meant dance routines, which we'd spend hours and hours rehearsing, usually at Pineapple Dance Studios in Covent Garden.

It never came easily to me, the dancing side of things. I found it hard to pick up, no doubt partly because I was always wearing a baggy day-glo shirt and a cheesy grin, but I'm better when we do it these days. On the 2020 series of Saturday Night Takeaway, we did a routine with Britain's Got Talent street dancers Twist and Pulse and, although it took plenty of practice, I was really pleased with how it went – and all without a cheesy grin in sight.

One of the other features of our pop career was our incredible versatility – we could make fools of ourselves in Britain, mainland Europe AND the Far East. Germany, in

– What do you mean other 20-year-olds don't take a hamper and fruit bowl on picnics with them? –

'No *you're* wearing matching shirts.' –

– Filming the 'U Krazy Katz' video in 1995. Because nothing says Krazy like dressing up as Victorian chimney sweeps. –

particular, was a country where we often seemed to put our foot in it.

The record company were forever reminding us that, 'After the US, Germany is the second biggest music market in the world – break Germany and you've got it made.'

You won't be surprised to hear that, in PJ & Duncan terms, Germany remained very much unbroken.

But it certainly wasn't for a lack of trying. On promotional duties for Top Katz, we were booked to appear on the *Bravo Super Show,* which was the German equivalent of the *Smash Hits Poll Winners Party.* It was a huge arena gig in front of 30,000 people and a massive TV audience, where a variety of pop acts would perform a song or two each. Every time we saw someone from the record company, at a TV show, a magazine shoot, a radio interview, we were told '*Bravo Super Show* is a huge deal'. I'm not sure how they managed the Herculean task of getting two British unknowns booked on to such a massive show, but somehow, they did it and we were off to the Super-ist show in all of Deutschland.

It came to the big day and we were ready to fly out to Germany. And then disaster struck – our flight was delayed. At first it was only by an hour, which meant we could still make the timings work for our big appearance. Then the flight was delayed by another hour and, eventually, a third hour. Our manager was on the phone to the Bravo Super Show people and they were very reassuring, saying, 'Don't worry, we can put their performance back' . . . but in German. But after the third delay, it was getting to the point where if they'd put our performance back any further, we'd have been the headline act.

And, trust me, PJ & Duncan were NOT going to be the headline act at the *Bravo Super Show*.

Eventually, we took off and time was very, very tight, but we were told we could still make it to the gig. On landing, we were greeted by our German artist liaison officer, a guy called Axel. Axel was tall, with shoulder-length hair, cowboy boots, a leather jacket and, the *pièce de résistance*, a tie with piano keys on.

I'm not saying Axel owned all of David Hasselhoff's albums, I'm just not saying he didn't own them.

Anyway, the man with the piano tie had a plan – there was no time to wait for our luggage, we were going to jump straight in a car and head for the arena.

But there was one problem – we didn't have our show clothes. We never performed without our show clothes, they made us feel like pop stars and, in that department, we needed all the help we could get. We were still dressed for a flight – both in black Adidas tracksuit bottoms, me in a blue hoodie, Dec in a black one.

Classic nineties pop star flight attire.

We told Axel we couldn't perform in the clothes we were wearing, but he assured us our luggage would follow in a separate car and we could get changed just before we went on, so we set off for the arena.

That journey was incredible; it was like being in a high-speed presidential motorcade. We sailed through every security barrier going and, all the while, the clock was ticking and Axel was saying, 'We can do this, we can do this!', while his piano tie swished in the breeze from the open car window.

Eventually, we arrived at the venue with seconds to spare, leapt out of the car and said, 'Right, where are our show clothes?'

Axel told us they hadn't arrived, and that there was no choice – we'd have to go on as we were, or miss the gig.

The situation was black and white.
   Much like the keys on his piano tie.

We'd been out of the car about 14 seconds when a technician handed us a microphone each and, with no make-up and wearing the clothes we'd flown in, we went on stage and performed in front of 30,000 screaming German teenagers.

And do you know what? It actually went pretty well; we got a good response and we'd performed at the biggest show in the 'second biggest market outside of the US'.

As we came off stage in our black tracksuit bottoms and blue and black hoodies, we were handed our luggage. We opened it up and there were our show clothes:

Two pairs of red Adidas tracksuit bottoms, a yellow hoodie and an orange hoodie.

We were very different off stage to on stage.

Incredibly, that wasn't our only experience with Bravo magazine, the German version of Smash Hits. In October 1995, we released 'U Krazy Kats', which in case you'd forgotten was the second single from Top Katz. Sure, we were into cats, but we were damned if we were going to spell them like everyone else did, we were completely crazy.

Or, to be more accurate, kompletely krazy.
   As part of the promotion, we were scheduled to do an

interview and photoshoot for *Bravo* and they wanted to do it in Newcastle. There was a real buzz about the city at the time – the football team were doing well in Europe (google it, kids, I'm not making this up) and the plan was that the article would have us visiting our old schools and our beloved St James' Park, scene of our first match together.

Newcastle United 1 Swindon Town 1, Boxing Day, 1990. I can smell that heady combination of stale urine, Regal king size and hot Bovril like it was yesterday.

But things got slightly tricky when our record label told us about the other part of the magazine article, an 'At home with PJ & Duncan' photoshoot. Or, as you'd say in German, 'Fotoshooting Zu Hause bei PJ und Duncan'.

Told you he had an aptitude for languages.

Or an aptitude for Google Translate.
    The idea was that we'd do the shoot in the flat we shared in Newcastle, but there was just one tiny problem with an article based around the flat we shared in Newcastle.

We didn't share a flat in Newcastle.
    But the first rule of journalism is: Never let the facts get in the way of a good story.

Pretty sure that's the total opposite of the first rule of journalism, but go on.

Our management were worried that Bravo, the largest teen magazine in the second biggest market outside of the US, would pull the article if it didn't feature the 'At home with . . .' element. We thought, 'No problem, we'll just find a flat and pretend we live in it.' You might think that seems like a silly idea, but you'd be wrong. It was actually a phenomenally stupid idea. In the end, we turned to the only people we could – our families.

In 1995, my mam's boyfriend had a flat he lived in with his son. It wasn't easy, but I eventually talked him into letting us use the flat for the photoshoot, and the two of them also agreed they wouldn't be home when it all happened.

We'd come up with an ingenious plan to convince the German magazine that we lived there, which was to get there before them, have a quick look around the place and then leave some of our stuff lying about. I can't remember, but I imagine the 'stuff' was probably some oversized American sportswear and possibly the match programme from Newcastle versus Swindon, but our plan went awry—

Excellent use of 'awry', by the way.

Nothing but plans ever go awry, do they? You never hear of a lasagne that went 'awry', do you?

This story's going to go 'awry' with any more interruptions like that.

As I was saying, our plan went awry because we got there later than we'd hoped, and we ended up arriving at the same time as the *Bravo* magazine gang. Not a great start to the shoot – we needed to sell records wherever we could, which meant there was a lot riding on this feature.

As we headed into the flat with them, our hearts were racing, and we already had the distinct feeling this might not go brilliantly.

To set the scene for you: the place was a two-bedroomed flat and the minute we started the guided tour for the German journalist, the plan began to fall apart. 'This is my room,' I proudly announced as I walked into my mam's boyfriend's room. It had a wardrobe that included a suede jacket and a pair of Kicker boots that screamed 'the 1980s'. Everything in the room, from the bedspread to the wallpaper, said, 'A middle-aged father of one lives here and definitely not Newcastle's most dynamic pop duo.'

I did the only thing I could and ushered them out of 'Ant's' room and offered them a cup of tea, but, as soon as we got into the kitchen, I had to open every single drawer and cupboard in the place to find what I needed. And then came five words that made my blood run cold: 'Where is your room, Dec?'

I immediately started to frantically point Dec in the right direction, hoping I couldn't be seen.

Once I'd finally worked out Ant's game of bedroom charades, I told them to follow me and, with the journalist and the photographer in tow, I headed down the corridor to 'my' room. I confidently opened the door to reveal a sight that, to this day, I'll never forget:

A He-Man bedspread, Airfix planes hanging from the ceiling and a toy castle on top of the chest of drawers.

I offered a weak smile and said, 'I'm still a kid at heart!'

The journalist surveyed the scene, then looked me right in the eye and said, 'This is not your flat, is it?'

I think that was the last time we had any contact with Bravo magazine. Right there and then, we said 'Auf Wiedersehen' to our chances of ever cracking the 'second biggest music market in the world'.

After the runaway mediocrity of our second album (number 46 in the UK album charts, thanks for asking), things needed to change for our third one – and change they did.

In 1997, we released The Cult Of Ant And Dec, which, most crucially of all, saw us changing our names to Ant and Dec.

We thought long and hard about becoming known as Ant and Dec, but, in the end, one thing convinced us it was the right decision.

They are our names.
   Although I still think Dec and Ant is just as catchy.

I'll tell you what I told your solicitor when he sent me that letter – it's alphabetical.

As part of our 'new direction', we also underwent a drastic and disastrous image change. The whole reason for the makeover was a photoshoot with legendary photographer Rankin, who was, and still is, one of the coolest and most sought-after photographers in the world. The idea for the shoot was that we were trying to 'age up' and leave the world of cheesy pop behind for good.

Next thing we know we're sent to see a hairdresser, but it wasn't in some exclusive, high-end salon, but at her flat. She shaved my head and then moved on to dyeing Dec's hair, which involved him bending over her bath.

Looking back, alarm bells should have been ringing when I saw her reading the instructions on the back of the bottle. I was thinking, 'I'm not really sure she knows what she's doing here.' Then she washed my hair, dried it with a towel and ta-da!

And by 'ta-da', he means his hair was dyed ginger.

And not just any ginger, a shade of ginger I still haven't seen on any human's head since.

On the plus side, the shoot and working with Rankin was a rare thrill. Not least because, unlike all our previous photoshoots, we could put some of our personality and humour into it. The two of us were wearing Hawaiian shirts and fake plastic chests that had six-packs on them, all while we stood in a paddling pool.

It was supposed to be a cheeky dig at the kind of boy-band images people like our sometime next-door neighbour Peter Andre were peddling at the time (no offence, Peter, you always did it way better than we did) and we loved it.

The Cult Of Ant And Dec actually did a lot better than its predecessor (number 15, thanks again for asking), but, despite that, it was becoming clear that our music career was reaching a natural conclusion. Although, even as things were winding down, there was one thing we had left.

Hope.

A long-standing contractual agreement to do a tour of the Far East.

Oh yeah. I always get those two mixed up.

We had also hosted quite a few TV shows of our own by this point, so we were hoping that after we'd honoured our commitment to the Far East tour, there might be new TV projects on the horizon when we got back.

We started the tour in Tokyo, where we completely rejected the joys of sushi or any other local cuisine in favour of the nearest American diner, which on this trip was a rib restaurant called 'Tony Roma's A Place For Ribs'.

*Every night on that tour, we'd have the same conversation
with our Japanese artist liaison officer:*

'Excuse me, Ant and Dec, have you had any thoughts about
where you would like to dine this evening?'
'Tony Roma's.'
'Again?'
'Yes please.'
'You know you have been there the last three nights?'
'Yes. Tony Roma's please.'

Our philosophy was less 'Travel broadens the mind' and
more 'Travels broadens the waistline . . . ideally with ribs
every night'.

After that we moved on to Indonesia, where we'd
been booked to perform at the Hard Rock Cafe in Jakarta
– obvious, really, considering we were a hard-rock
band. Before the gig, we were scheduled to do a press
conference.

*We were accompanied by our Indonesian artist liaison
representative, which is someone employed by the record
company who co-ordinates where you go and what you
do. When you're in Indonesia. The guy we were given was
basically a PJ & Duncan superfan, and from here on in we'll
refer to him as Superfan – partly to preserve his anonymity,
but mainly because we can't remember his name.*

*He was also what's known in showbusiness circles as a right
pain in the arse. When we'd drive to gigs in the same car, he'd
often just be staring at us longingly. It was all very strange.*

But, undeterred, the three of us made our way to the press
conference and, en route, Superfan told us that when we
got there, we should sing a capella for the press.

We told him in no uncertain terms: 'We can't sing a capella.'

That sentence also works without the words 'a capella'.

He said, 'Backstreet Boys did it here' – as if that would suddenly change our minds – but we were adamant, we weren't singing a capella. As you know by now, we mainly mimed to a backing track when we performed.

At first, Superfan wasn't having any of it – he just wasn't listening to us telling him he wouldn't be listening to us – but eventually he gave up, just as we arrived at the venue for the press conference. It was a boiling-hot day but the room we were taken into did at least have air-conditioning.

I mean, it was broken, but we were reliably informed it did have air-conditioning.

The assembled journalists didn't look happy from the get-go, which is hardly surprising. Imagine spending years training to be a professional journalist and then you get stuck in a sweatbox to put questions to PJ & Duncan . . . or Ant and Dec, as we were by then. And the reception they gave us was the total opposite of the room we were stuck in.– frosty. But eventually we managed to win them over, mainly thanks to a 'joke' I always made in the Far East – the observation that Dec looked like Michael J. Fox, who apparently was very popular over there.

I'm honoured to have worked with such a gifted comic mind for 30 years.

By the end of the press conference, though, we had them eating out of our hands. The journalists were even giving us a round of applause as we walked out – although that may have just been to create ventilation – but we were literally at the door when we heard a voice we recognised:

'AntandDec, before you go, maybe you could sing a cappella for the press?'

It was Superfan. Again. He always said our names as one.

Before we knew what was happening, the entire room was shouting, 'A capella, a capella, a capella!' and they wouldn't stop. It was agonising. There was only one thing we could do.

Run.

You thought we were going to say 'Sing a capella', didn't you?

As we made our escape, the press started to boo. Very loudly. I tried to say something about Dec looking like Michael J. Fox, but they'd turned on us. It was one of the most humiliating experiences of our music career – and this is from the people who brought you 'Our Fake Flat' and 'Dec's Ginger Hair'.

We went back to a dressing room they'd given us at the Hard Rock Cafe and we were furious. I'm suddenly aware as I'm typing this that it sounds like the kind of hidden-camera stunt we'd pull years later on *Saturday Night Takeaway* in our Undercover segment, but we were livid at the time. And then there was a knock at the door. Still fuming, I answered to find Superfan standing there. I expected an apology, but all I got was, 'Can I get my coat and my bag?' I wanted to give him a lot more than that.

I threw his bag and coat into the corridor (rock 'n' roll!) and we told him we wouldn't be doing the gig and that we never, ever wanted to hear from him again.

– The Rankin photoshoot.
Eagle-eyed readers will
notice that they aren't our
real torsos. –

– Mock us all you like, but we knew how
to rock an autumnal colour palette. –

– After the rebrand we were definitely
cooler. Ahem. –

Then we went back to the hotel and took a decision that required serious balls. We played tennis. I'm not sure why we did it, neither of us has ever really been into tennis, but the court was on the roof of the hotel and it gave us the chance to let off some steam. We'd just started the first game when we heard a voice.

'AntandDec, I'm sorry, AntandDec, please come to the Hard Rock Cafe, AntandDec.'

It was . . . well, you know by now. His mouth was poking through the mesh at the side of the tennis court and we both just burst out laughing.

Once the laughter had subsided, we told him in no uncertain terms that he'd embarrassed us, we'd been humiliated, and we'd have to be pretty desperate to do the gig after that farce.

And then? Well, we did the gig.

When we got back home, Telstar offered us another record deal and our manager at the time said, 'It's not a great deal, but it's a deal' – so we went back into the studio and started work on some new material. A few days in, we took a taxi back to our flat and had a conversation that would change the rest of our lives. It went like this:

'I'm not enjoying this any more.'
'Neither am I.'
'Shall we knock it on the head?'
'Aye.'

And that was it, there and then, we stopped being pop stars. And in all those years of the roadshows, the magazine shoots, the radio interviews and the TV performances, we'd never even got near to having a number one single. The closest we'd got was 'Let's Get Ready To Rhumble' hitting number nine.

That was until, 19 years later, when something very, very strange happened – but more of that later.

Ooh, you little tease.

3

KIDS'

TV

So, we'd handed in our badges to Pop Star HQ and decided to give TV our full attention. We'd already had a fair bit of presenting experience during our pop 'career' and even had a few of our own shows made.

The first of them was called – and get ready for this – *The Ant and Dec Show.* I know, we really broke the mould when it came to titles. It was for CBBC and we made two series, in 1995 and 1996. We even won a Children's BAFTA.

Our main memory of The Ant and Dec Show was the first time we worked with proper comedy writers. There were (I think) five of them and they included Dean Wilkinson, a fellow Northeasterner and someone we worked with for the next seven years, and Simon Heath, who is now the CEO of World Productions and the executive producer of Line of Duty.

Where did it all go right, Simon?

And a bloke who was constantly risqué, disruptive and inappropriate.

His name was David Walliams.
   I wonder what his first impressions of those two young upstarts from Newcastle were?

DAVID WALLIAMS: 'I was really starstruck by Ant and Dec the first time I met them. I was a big pop music fan and had seen them on *Byker Grove* too. I wasn't immediately sure they'd be the next Morecambe and Wise, but as we got to know each other, I began to see there was something special about them. They had charisma, they worked hard, and they didn't have any vanity. They were also generous with each other, as performers; it wasn't as if one of them wanted all the laughs, they were a real partnership.

Initially, I wondered what I'd have in common with these two lads from Newcastle, but we all shared a deep love of comedy and we bonded over that.'

Did you hear that, reader? 'Starstruck'.

David led a very sheltered life in those days . . .

I have so many fond memories of working with David back then. As you'd expect, his scripts were really funny – and there was one thing that was particularly hilarious in every single script of David's.

He drew tiny penises all over them. David, or at least 1995 David Walliams, loved drawing tiny penises on things. It got to the point that whenever his scripts were dished out in a meeting, you started to look for the phallic artwork.

It wasn't so much 'Where's Wally?' as 'Where's Willy?'

DAVID: 'The thing about me is I'm very mischievous and I'm easily bored. And so I took any opportunity I could to make them laugh, especially in front of the "grown-ups".

And they both had that mischievous glint in their eye too, they still do. I had a real kinship with them over that. We felt like the naughty kids in the class.'

David's right, we were the naughty kids at the back of the class, but he started it, sir, we were just laughing at the pictures.

Anyway, aside from the tiny penises—

Which, coincidentally, was also David's nickname for us two.

—David's scripts always pushed the envelope and in meetings, you could rely on him to make completely inappropriate jokes that were never going to make it on to a kids' TV show.

The other thing David did was write himself into all the sketches. I remember a Starsky and Hutch parody David wrote called 'Retro Cops', where our characters had to stop a vicar who was driving down the street. David obviously 'volunteered' to play the part of vicar and, when it came to the day, he arrived with his own comedy glasses and novelty teeth.

The novelty gnashers had a tiny penis drawn on each individual tooth, but fortunately you couldn't really see it on screen. Only joking.

The cameras started rolling and the director yelled 'Action!' and, as planned, David the goofy vicar drove the car into shot.

But unbeknownst to everyone on set, just before filming began, David had made one key wardrobe adjustment, designed to show off another part of his 'repertoire'. We stopped the car and dragged the vicar out, only to reveal David wasn't wearing any trousers. Basically, his top half was worshipping the Good Lord, while the bottom half was ready to dance with the devil.

- David Walliams and two schoolchildren
from Newcastle. -

- 'Keep smiling,
someone in a red
jumper's trying to
nick our BAFTA.' -

- Ant inadvertently invents photobombing
in the mid nineties. -

We lost it laughing. The director was furious, which just made us laugh even more. The producers had to constantly rein David in on that show and we absolutely loved it.

> DAVID: 'As a frustrated performer myself back then, I never shied away from getting a laugh, even if it was a cheap laugh.'

If you ask me, a cheap laugh is one of the best laughs you can get.

And, of course, ours and David's paths have continued to cross over the last couple of decades.

That's another one of his nicknames for us, 'A couple of decades'.

At least I think that's what he said . . .

Not just on Britain's Got Talent and on Saturday Night Takeaway either; we've even run into each other in Los Angeles, California. In 2007, we made a TV show in America called Wanna Bet? and, by complete coincidence, a certain Mr Walliams was in town and booked into the same hotel as us.

That is a coincidence, someone with the same surname as our friend David Walliams being booked into the hotel.

No, it was David Walliams, you were there, remember?

Oh yeah, sorry.

One morning, I was in my room ironing my shirt for a meeting when my breakfast arrived. I opened the door, took in my food and then spotted a man I recognised standing in the doorway of the room opposite mine. He was wearing a

*loosely tied robe and making the kind of risqué remarks I
remembered from CBBC back in 1995.*

Wow, who was it?

*It was David Walliams! Will you keep up? After saying how
impressed he was that I ironed my own shirts, he added,
'Well, I know where you live now!' and then sashayed back
into his room like only David can. Later that day, after our
meetings had finished, we got back to the hotel and the
receptionist said, 'Mr McPartlin, housekeeping says there is a
letter for you in your room.' I went straight up, excited to see
who'd written to me, but when I opened the door to my room,
all I saw on the floor was a room service menu. But this was no
ordinary room service menu – it had penises drawn all over it.*

Wow, who would do such a thing?

I'll swing for you in a minute.
    *To be fair to David, his art had really moved on since
the nineties – the penises were all sorts of shapes and sizes
now and they even included a bit of text that said things like
'David's penis', 'Ant's penis', 'Dec's penis'.*
    *What followed was a week of me and David putting
increasingly rude drawings under each other's doors –
housekeeping must have thought we were conducting some
sort of illicit affair.*

> DAVID: 'Basically, give me any chance to be
> naughty and silly and I'll take it.'

Me and you both, David.
    *Despite all of this, I'd like to assure everyone that my
friendship with David has always been based on nothing
more than mutual respect.*

And penis drawings.

And penis drawings.

Now, where were we? Oh yes, kids' TV. We'd done *The Ant and Dec Show* on BBC and then we went on to host some shows on Channel 4. We did some stints on *The Big Breakfast* and also made a series called *Ant and Dec: Unzipped* that was essentially a slightly more grown-up version of *The Ant and Dec Show*. And, by slightly more grown-up, I mean it was on at 6pm, rather than 4.35.

I don't know if our audience was busy watching the Six O'Clock News on BBC1, but Unzipped didn't return for a second series. So we started working on some new ideas through our production company, the imaginatively titled 'Ant and Dec Productions'. Our plan was to move away from kids' TV and into grown-up telly . . . although using words like 'grown-up telly' probably explains why we didn't immediately take Saturday nights by storm.

It's incredible now to look back and think that, at 22 years old, the two of us had our own TV production company. At the time, we'd seen Chris Evans make a big success of his company, Ginger Productions, and that knowledge, coupled with a healthy dollop of youthful arrogance, meant that we went for it.

We set the company up with Zenith North (who used to make Byker Grove), guided by two of the executives, Ivan Rendall and Peter Murphy. They told us that if we wanted to create our own ideas, this was the best way to do it. And just like my drama teacher Lyn Spencer and Dec's Cruddas MAD group ten years earlier, they gave us the encouragement we needed to get started. Without that, we'd never have done it.

Each month, we'd have a board meeting – although I don't remember them lasting very long at the beginning, because we weren't making any TV shows. But throughout, me and Ant always had two things: a strong work ethic and a passion for television. And things started looking up for the company when we had an idea for a music show.

Our plan was to 'steal' the official chart from the BBC, who used it on Top of the Pops and the Sunday night Top 40 show on Radio 1. We'd found out from a spy—

Not a real spy. They've got better stuff to do.

—that the TV contract for the chart was up for renewal soon, so we wanted to hijack it and then make a new chart show, hosted by, yes, you've guessed it, the CEOs of Ant and Dec Productions. And we wanted to do this on Saturday mornings on ITV.

Like we said, we were 22 years old.

The best thing about our plan was how we executed it. We put together a pitch document with our then producer Conor McAnally and put it in a briefcase, then handcuffed that briefcase to a security guard and sent him to ITV. We told him to walk in and tell them, 'I've got a special delivery for [Director of Programmes] David Liddiment', and instructed him not to leave until he'd handed over the document.

It's like the worst Bond film ever made, isn't it?

Incredibly, our security guard actually managed to get the documents to David Liddiment. David opened the briefcase, read the documents and, drum roll . . .

Decided he wasn't interested in the show.

Although two positives did come out of the whole thing: firstly, David loved the 'mischief' of it, got us in for a meeting and we ended up making a different music show for him; and, secondly, him and the security guard became great friends and remain close to this day.

To cut a long story short, the programme ITV wanted us to make was cd:uk, but there was one condition – they also wanted us to host a two-hour Saturday morning kids' show before it, made by our company. For two 22-year-olds to be offered three hours of terrestrial TV per week to host for an incredible 52 weeks a year was the kind of opportunity that only a damn fool would turn down.

So we turned it down.

At first.

Then we had several conversations with ITV's controller of children's programmes, Nigel Pickard. Nigel explained that this was the perfect chance for us to learn our presenting trade away from the spotlight – we'd get to host hours and hours of live TV, wear an earpiece, do sketches, games and interviews; it was basically a boot camp for what we do now. Everything he said made complete sense.

So naturally, we turned it down.

Again.

At the time, we were trying to step away from the cheesy world of teen pop and kids' TV – and we thought hosting a Saturday morning kids' show would take us back into that world.

We could not have been more wrong.

God knows why, but Nigel, aka St Nigel (the patron saint of TV presenters who make daft decisions), persisted and, in the end, we finally said yes. And from that day, *sm:tv*, a two-hour live kids' magazine show, and *cd:uk*, a one-hour music show, were born. If TV shows can be born. Which, of course, they can't.

We didn't know it at the time, but this also turned out to be the start of our long-term relationship with ITV.

Fast-forward to 29 August 1998 when sm:tv and cd:uk launched, hosted by two blokes called Ant and Dec and a young lady by the name of Cat Deeley. We'd considered a number of co-hosts, but Cat stood head and shoulders above the competition.

She also stood head and shoulders above us two, which was why we often made her sit down when we did the show.

Cat was – and is – smart, funny and, most importantly of all, someone who loves taking the p*** out of us two. The three of us really clicked off screen; we loved hanging out together, even when we weren't at work. Although Cat did have a few blind spots about TV . . .

CAT DEELEY: *'I was so naive back then, but ignorance is bliss. Before the first show, I actually asked Ant if my nan would be able to see it in Birmingham!*

I'd been working at MTV for two years, but Ant and Dec had been in the entertainment industry since they were kids; they were much more savvy and so I'm sure they felt the pressure much more than me. And this show was their 'baby', they had been involved from its conception.'

We certainly had, Catherine Noddy Slade Deeley (which is her actual full name. Well, it's the actual full name we made up for her, being from Birmingham and all). Anyway, the show ended up being a baby we all raised together. And when August 1998 arrived, we went on air with three new presenters

– Some of the more highbrow
moments on *sm:tv*. –

on a channel that had traditionally struggled against the BBC on Saturday mornings, and a lot of people thought our show might be a disaster. But we showed those people.

Yep, we showed them they were absolutely right.

> CAT: *'Our saving grace was that we were being beaten so badly in the ratings that no one was watching, giving us time to find our feet. Thank goodness no one was watching those first shows, they were pretty bad. Stinkers, in fact!'*

'Stinkers'? Hang on, those first shows weren't . . . no, actually, Cat's right, they were stinkers.

Even now, there is a huge affection for sm:tv, but a lot of people forget that it had very difficult beginnings. When it started, it had none of the things people remember so fondly – Chums, Wonkey Donkey, Challenge Ant – or presenters who knew what they were doing.

Cat was great, don't get me wrong, but the show just didn't really know what it was and the kids watching . . . all three of them . . . smelt that a mile off. The BBC had Zoe Ball and Jamie Theakston doing *Live and Kicking*, while ITV had Ant, Dec and Cat doing 'Live and Not Quite Sure What We Were Doing'.

The problem was that we thought we were too cool for school, so we spent the whole morning building up to the music show, *cd:uk*, when we should have focused on entertaining young kids in the first part of the show. They were in charge of the remote control and, if you got them early, they'd keep watching all morning.

For months on end, we got slaughtered by the BBC in the ratings, and, before we knew it, it was almost Christmas and it looked like Santa might not be the only one getting the sack.

We had so much riding on it back then too: we'd both just moved out of our shared, rental flat and ploughed most of our savings into buying our first houses and, if the show failed, we wouldn't be able to pay our mortgages, which made it even more stressful.

But against all reasonable evidence, St Nigel of ITV didn't cancel the show. And then, a miracle happened – something that saved us, something that over the years has saved a million showbiz careers. And that thing was pantomime.

Earlier that year, when we were in that hinterland between failing pop stars and failing kids' TV presenters, we'd signed up to do Snow White and the Seven Dwarfs at the Sunderland Empire. I think they asked Sir Ian McKellen first, but he was busy.

We played those most illustrious of roles, Dame Dolly Doughnut's nephews (me neither). Across the course of a couple of months (during a lot of which we were also doing the Saturday morning show) we learnt a lesson that changed everything.

We learnt how to talk to our audience. We'd spent months trying to pretend we were some sort of cool music show and had ignored the people the show was meant to be aimed at – children. But performing to a theatre full of kids day after day after day quickly enabled us to work out what made them laugh. Which, as any parent will tell you, is: big props, daft songs and toilet humour. Lots and lots of toilet humour.

In the New Year, we took that intricate piece of invaluable audience data—

Fart noises. He's basically talking about fart noises.

–and changed the whole Saturday morning show. We added big silly games, sketches where we dressed up, and generally threw ourselves into the task of trying to make kids like the show. And guess what? Slowly but surely, it worked. We started getting better ratings, the show got better, and it finally felt like we had a fighting chance of surviving on TV.

Worth mentioning again, this was mainly thanks to fart noises.

Over the next year or so, the show went from strength to strength. We became closer with Cat, which showed on screen, and, most importantly of all, we started to put some good stuff on air and actually had fun hosting it. We've got so many happy memories of doing things like Splattoon, All Hands on Dec, Captain Justice, Dec Says, Eat My Goal, the Postbag dance, Challenge Ant, Wonkey Donkey and Fart Attack with Neil Pumpcannon.

It was pretty highbrow stuff.
    So much changed when the show became a success, not least the fact that we could stop fretting about paying the mortgage.

We also signed with a new management company, James Grant Management – now YMU – who we're still with today. And they gave us some great advice – that we should simplify things. They suggested we stop getting so involved in the production company and concentrate on making the show. We did just that and, overnight, life became a lot easier. We had none of the board meetings or grown-up stuff to deal with. We could just focus all our energies on making sm:tv and cd:uk as good as they could possibly be.

And with that kind of stability, making the show became a joy – and full of the kind of little rituals and routines anyone enjoys when they work with the same people week in, week out for years on end.

I always thought our relationship on screen mirrored our relationship off screen – wonder what Cat thought?

> CAT: *'I think our relationship on screen mirrored our relationship off screen. When the show began, the lads already had an established relationship, but you can't hothouse friendship or chemistry, it develops, if you're lucky, over the passage of time.'*

And lucky we were, because our friendship developed into something really special.

Show day was a great example of the kind of routines that still exist on the shows we make today. We'd get picked up at 5am and then get to the London Studios – a building we had to ourselves because it was a Saturday – and meet Cat in the canteen at around 6am. The three of us would have a bacon roll and a chat, talking about what we'd done on our quiet Friday night in.

And a lot of that Friday night in was spent trying to learn the script that had been taking shape since Monday morning. One of the main methods we employed for *cd:uk* was to take home a batch of blank cue cards and handwrite each separate section of the script onto them. And if you lost any of those cue cards, you were in big trouble – there was no autocue, it's generally not used on Saturday morning shows, so they were our lifeline to keeping the show going smoothly. Well, maybe not smoothly, but keeping it going.

After our bacon rolls, we'd go off and get changed, get made up and then, by 7.30, we were on set, rehearsing the show until 9.25 when it went live – which was when the mayhem really started.

There were so many different sketches, characters and costumes that it was incredibly hectic. There were a lot of quick changes, often in the corridor outside the studio because there wasn't time to go to the dressing room. I remember the outfit for my character Captain Justice (a superhero who was the 'guardian of consumer rights') being a right kick bollocks scramble in particular.

And because of the layout of the London Studios, those frantic corridor costume changes happened right next to the same canteen we'd been having our bacon rolls in three hours earlier. Except by this time, the place was teeming with pop stars and celebrities who'd come to be on the show that week.

So you might be half-naked, frantically trying to put on an ill-fitting spandex superhero suit while waving to S Club 7, Billie Piper or Victoria Beckham, as they were getting ready to appear in that week's episode of Chums.

Chums was, without doubt, our favourite thing about *sm:tv*. It was a homage to—

(Rip-off of)

—the legendary American sitcom *Friends* and the idea was simple – me, Ant and Cat shared a flat. Ant's character was a combination of Joey and Chandler, while Cat and I had a flirtatious Ross and Rachel, will-they-wont-they?, relationship. We did it live and it was like a little sitcom every week, often with co-stars who were reading their lines for the first time when it was on air. It was always full of slapstick comedy and *double entendres* and we never got through one without someone cracking up laughing.

We had some amazing co-stars over the years, including Kylie Minogue, Sting, Sir Tom Jones, Jamiroquai and the Spice Girls, all culminating in an incredible, star-studded, final 'wedding' episode. And, of course, the reason we had those amazing co-stars was because they were already in the studio to perform on cd:uk, which meant we were never short of talent to share the screen with. One of the best things about cd:uk was that, as the show became more successful, we got some legendary acts on, people like Blur, Foo Fighters, Paul McCartney and Oasis.

The show became the place to be if you were a music act with a new release to promote. One of the big things we had going for us was that record companies knew that if their artists appeared on *cd:uk* on a Saturday morning, then that afternoon kids would go out shopping and buy their single: it was the perfect shop window.

There was one guest from that time who stands out – former Guns N' Roses guitarist Slash.

I was a huge Guns N' Roses fan as a teenager. I was over the moon when we heard he was coming . . . although I felt distinctly under the moon when the producers decided Cat, not me and Ant, should interview him. When it came to the interview, us two were in one part of the studio, probably doing a competition to win S Club 7's hair straighteners or something, when Slash arrived. And let me tell you, he was everything you wanted him to be - top hat, shades, that hair. I was well jealous of Cat.

- *sm:tv* rehearsals and a rare 'in front of the scenes' shot. -

by George was ecstatic to appearing on the show. -

- Our last ever rehearsal in 2001.
This was our fantastic production
team, including 'Ol' Double Denim
Donnelly' himself. -

CAT: 'Slash finally sat down next to me 20 seconds before the interview. He'd been up all night and had quite possibly rolled straight into the studio. As the floor manager counted down from ten to one, Slash lit a cigarette, which the floor manager took out of his mouth at the last second.'

Sparking up a fag in the studio of a kids' TV show — classic Slash.

As always happened on the show, when Cat was doing an interview we still wore our earpieces, so we could hear everyone in the gallery. We couldn't hear Cat, but we could hear the producer, who was our good friend Phil Mount, and the director.

Side note: Our earpieces are how the producer and director can talk to us from the gallery, or control room. That means they can remind us which camera we're on or what's coming up next, among other things.

So, the Slash interview started, and we waited patiently to do our competition at the end of it. Then, suddenly, absolute pandemonium broke out in our earpieces. The first time I knew something was up was when I heard Phil screaming, 'We've had a f**k! We've had a f**k!'

I immediately thought, 'What on earth are they getting up to in that gallery?'

Then the next thing I heard was, 'We've had a b**w j*b! We've had a b**w j*b!'

I thought they were having some sort of orgy in there.
    Then Phil started talking to us two in our ears. He told us that Slash had been swearing and that they'd cut the

interview short. They were coming to us two any second and we needed to apologise, which we did, although it wasn't an easy thing to do.

Mainly because we were in hysterics, which made doing a 'sorry face' quite tricky. It turned out Slash had discussed how his rhino iguana 'bit the f**k out of him' and then proceeded to scotch a rumour that he once got 'a b**w j*b in a bar'.

Understandably, the show received a ton of complaints and it made a lot of headlines, not that me, Ant or Cat were especially bothered.

CAT: *'Looking back now, I'm so glad he wasn't a letdown. He's Slash, not Mickey Mouse. We booked Slash and we certainly got Slash.'*

Mickey Mouse would probably have smoked and sworn less, but we were still glad we got Slash.

By far the biggest band we had on cd:uk, though, were U2. We've both been huge fans for as long as we can remember, and we were thrilled when they agreed to come on in 2000 – and then even more thrilled when they asked us to nip into their dressing room before the show. We walked in nervously and the first exchange between us went like this:

Them: Hello you two.
Us: Hello U2.

And then Bono thanked us for having them; they said they were fans of the show, and they appreciated the fact we were introducing them to a new generation. We were dumbstruck – not only were we standing there talking to U2, but they were fans of the show. I was tempted to see if they fancied a quick game of Wonkey Donkey, but I decided against it. You won't be surprised to hear that their performance on the show was amazing – it felt like they were at the top of their game and, at the time, their track 'Beautiful Day' was the theme tune to ITV's Premier League show and they were everywhere.

The following week, we ran a competition to win tickets to U2 live at Slane Castle (in County Meath, about 30 miles from Dublin), with flights and accommodation thrown in, and on the spur of the moment, live on air, I said, 'And isn't this nice; Bono's said we can go too.'

And I chipped in with, 'Is that right? He's a lovely fella that Bono, isn't he?' We'd only said it for a laugh, but after the show Bono rang up, and what was it he called us?

The exact same nickname David Walliams has for us – a couple of decades.
   At least I think that's what Bono said, the phone signal wasn't great.

Then he said he supposed he'd have to invite us to the gig now. Not only that, but he paid for a bunch of our mates, including our *cd:uk* producer Phil Mount, to go over with us. It was a dream come true.

The weekend of the gig arrived and, well, let's just say, if Carlsberg did weekends, it would have been like this. We spent the afternoon sitting backstage with Sir Bob Geldof, watching England beat Germany 5–1.

Then we went out front to the VIP section to watch the gig, which was incredible, and at the after-show party, Bono even came over to say hello. However, after seeing him perform for two hours, we were in total awe and felt completely tongue-tied. As the world's biggest U2 fan, our producer Phil was particularly starstruck, but, despite that, he decided to break the conversational ice.

Clearly overawed by the whole situation, Phil looked at Bono and said:

'Thanks so much, Bono. It's been a beautiful day.'

Bono looked at Phil, trying to work out if he was taking the p***, Phil looked at us two apologetically, then Bono looked at us all, smiled and walked off.

I won't tell you exactly what we said to Phil afterwards, but one of Slash's favourite words was frequently used.

Making *sm:tv* and *cd:uk* was without doubt one of the most rewarding things we've ever done in our 30 years together, but, in 2001, we decided it was time to say goodbye to Saturday morning telly. The main reason for this was that *Pop Idol* had taken off and we'd soon be moving on to a hugely successful primetime Saturday night show, which would make it impossible to carry on in the mornings at the same time.

But that didn't make leaving *sm:tv* and *cd:uk* any easier.

It was one of the toughest decisions we've ever made, but once our minds were made up, we set about trying to make our farewell show on 1 December 2001 as memorable as it could possibly be. There were so many highlights from that final show, but the biggest of them all was the most star-studded episode of Chums we'd ever made. After three years of 'will-they-won't-they?' between Dec and Cat, the last episode saw them finally get together and get married. And the most starry of all the stars that studded that star-studded cast came in the shape of one of Cat's bridesmaids: Ms Mariah Carey.

Back then, the tabloids were always reporting that Mariah was the biggest diva in pop (unlike us, who had been the biggest divs in pop . . .) and, although we were thrilled she would be appearing in Chums, there was a part of us wondering if she might be hard work and not play along with the sketch.

But those worries disappeared in one phone call in the week running up to the show. It was a call taken by sm:tv producer, David Staite. He picked up to a number he didn't recognise and enjoyed the following exchange:

'Hi, David, it's Mariah Carey.'

'Er, um . . . Hi, Mariah.'

'I have a question for you – what colour is the wallpaper on the Chums set?'

'Pardon?'

'What colour is the wallpaper?'

'Purple, why?'

'I'm in Virgin Brides in Manchester, and I want to make sure I rent a bridesmaid's dress that clashes with the wallpaper – it'll look funnier then, won't it?'

'Er, yeah, it will, yeah.'

'Great – I'll get a blue one. See you Saturday!'

When it came to the day of the show, some of the team were still worried she might be high maintenance, but the minute she walked in carrying a plastic bag from Virgin Brides, we knew she'd be good as gold – and she was.

CAT: *'When we were waiting in the wings to make our entrance, Mariah actually dropped to her knees and fluffed up my dress. Then she looked up at me and said, 'You've gotta look your best sweetie . . . it's your wedding day!' She was brilliant!'*

I didn't know that! Good old Mariah!

Alongside Ms Carey's presence, we had goodbye messages from some incredible people – Bono, Sir Bobby Robson, Alan Shearer, Kylie Minogue, Paul McCartney, David Beckham and Sting were all on the list. I can safely say it's the only time the legendary Sir Bobby Robson appeared on the same 'bill' as Mariah Carey.

I'd promised myself I wouldn't get emotional, but I pretty much burst into tears during the last link. That show meant the absolute world to the pair of us and we'll never, ever forget what it gave us, what it taught us, and the friends we made along the way. Crucially, it had also done exactly what St Nigel of ITV said it would – it taught us our trade – and we still use so many of those skills when we're on TV now, almost 20 years later.

It also gave us a strange sensation, something we'd never experienced on a consistent basis – being proud of the work we were doing, and we've tried to recreate that on everything we've done since.

And then, of course, there was Cat; we loved every minute of sharing the screen with her. She's still the only person we've done that with in our three decades and we wouldn't have swapped her for anyone in the world.

CAT: *'I've never worked on a show like it. What the three of us had was way beyond a working relationship. I learnt so much from Ant and Dec and they were incredibly generous with me. We didn't just become a trio on screen, but in life.'*

I'm filling up here.

But after probably the most emotional farewell of our 30-year career, we made the move to Saturday night telly and embraced our biggest challenge yet.

Finding a tailor who could make suits in children's sizes.

I was going to say, 'Making a go of primetime TV', but yours works too.

– Rehearsing Chums. What do you mean,
'You actually did rehearsals?' –

– The big wedding and a real career
high . . . for Mariah Carey. –

DO NOT LEAVE LYING AROUND

SM:tv

Hosted FOR THE LAST TIME by
ANT & DEC & CAT
SMTV: Robbie Williams & Jonathan Wilkes, Jamiroquai
CDUK: Mariah Carey, Jamiroquai, Stereophonics,
Robbie Williams (post rec: Jennifer Lopez)

– Script for the last
ever show (tears stains
since dried). –

– Reunion with Cat in 2005 . . . –

– . . . and 2017. –

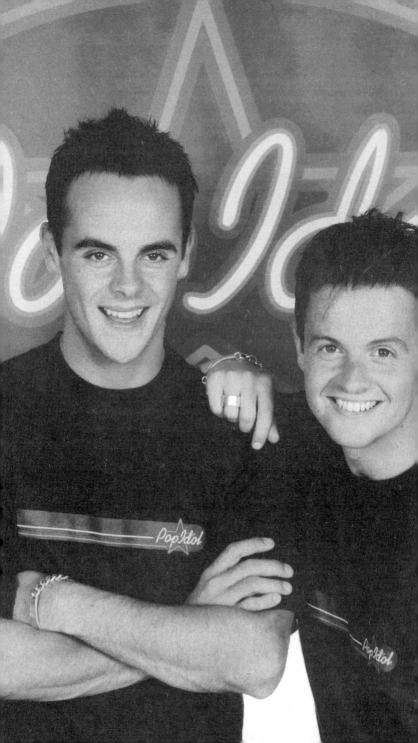

4

POP

IDOL

While we were still hosting an ITV show that started at 9.25am on a Saturday, the chance came up to do something completely and utterly different – host an ITV show that started at 7pm on a Saturday. That show was called Pop Idol *and, in many ways, it remains the most important job of our entire 30 years in telly.*

We'd already had a couple of goes at hosting big primetime Saturday night shows, with mixed results. In 1999, we made a programme for BBC1 called *Friends Like These*, which was a game show where friends competed against each other in various challenges. It did quite well, but it was pre-recorded and very heavily formatted, which meant we didn't get much of a chance to do the kind of stuff we loved – sketches, jokes and all-round mucking about.

The other Saturday night show we'd made was called Slap Bang *and it was on ITV in the summer of 2001, the same year we eventually left Saturday mornings. It was an attempt to recreate the mayhem of* sm:tv *on a Saturday night, but we quickly learnt that you need more than that in primetime. There was one moment in particular that taught us that lesson.*

It was when the bosses at ITV said, 'This show is terrible and no one's watching it, we're not doing any more episodes.'

We're very good at reading between the lines when it comes to stuff like that; it's just an instinct we have.

So, back to this little show called *Pop Idol*. I still remember us walking into reception at ITV with one of our managers, Paul Worsley, for the first meeting about it. Despite the failure of *Slap Bang*, we were still riding high with *sm:tv* and *cd:uk* and we took a seat while Paul signed us all in. After a couple of minutes of waiting, we were called over to collect our visitor passes, but there were only two — one for Paul and one for 'Anton Dec'.

It was so funny of the receptionist to pretend she'd never heard of us and thought we were some bloke called Anton Dec. And she loved a running joke — she kept up the hilarious pretence of not having a clue who we were every single time we visited ITV.

Classic banter.

We went into the meeting with two ITV big cheeses, David Liddiment (of handcuffed security guard fame) and Claudia Rosencrantz (Controller of Entertainment). They told us that after the smash-hit success of *Popstars* (a talent show where a panel of judges chose singers to make up a group), they were going to make a show about finding a solo artist. And there was a twist: for the first time ever, the public would choose the winner. Then they looked us square in the eye and said, 'We think the host should be Anton Dec.'

More classic banter.

Seriously, though, we bit their hand off (not literally, we'd never have worked again). I think the conversation went something like this:

ITV: It's called *Pop Idol* and, for the first time ever, the public choose the winner and . . .
Us: We'll do it.
ITV: Don't you want to know who the judges . . .
Us: When do we start?

And we never regretted that decision for a second. We were still only 25 at this point, but we'd been in the industry for 11 years and it felt like this was the chance we'd been

– The *Pop Idol* team ask, 'Is it technically a conga with six people?' –

– Pete Waterman, Kylie Minogue and
Simon Cowell. Sort of. –

– *Pop Idol* audition room: Be
cargo shorts were mandator

– The *Pop Idol* crew and another failed Sgt Pepper cover re-creation. –

waiting for. Of course, we'd have to adapt and evolve from what we'd been doing on Saturday mornings, but *Pop Idol* gave us a real shot at primetime. And, even better, it was an opportunity that didn't put us front and centre of the whole show, which meant a bigger, more mainstream audience could gradually get to know us.

Also, we had to do less work, which was nice.

Most excitingly of all, though, *Pop Idol* was the start of something completely new. This was before *The X Factor* and before *Britain's Got Talent* – there hadn't been a talent show on this scale, where the public chose the winner, and that was massive. It felt like something genuinely thrilling was happening.

It was also a show that started so many of the trends we're now so used to seeing in shows like that – hugging contestants after a triumphant audition, enjoying the more 'eccentric' performers, emotionally charged montages, and one other thing.

Some bloke called Simon Cowell.

These days, one of Simon's best-known catchphrases is 'I didn't like it . . . I loved it', and the moment we started working with him, well, let's just say, 'We didn't like him . . .'

That's it, we just didn't like him.

We're joking. We'd come across Simon in the early days of sm:tv when he was a record company executive. We even had a meeting with him about him creating the theme tune for sm:tv, which he wanted us to sing on.

SIMON COWELL: 'At the time, a lot of people were calling me about them, saying how much they were gonna be stars, *blah-blah-blah, so I just thought it's time for me to try to get in the Ant and Dec business.'*

We've been trying to get in the Ant and Dec business for years. For reasons that, quite frankly, escape me now, that early collaboration with Simon never happened, but we'd still run into him lots – he would come down to cd:uk with artists like Five and Girl Thing who were on his label. Back then, whenever we spoke to him about pop acts, he was rude, cutting and dismissive. It was an attitude that made us laugh. And an attitude that ultimately made him a multimillionaire. With hindsight, Pop Idol signified the start of our long-term relationship with Simon and, over the years, the three of us have been fortunate enough to work on some great shows together.

Simon was joined on the *Pop Idol* judging panel by music manager Nicki Chapman, DJ Dr Fox, music executive Pete Waterman and, of course, by his own ego, which took up three chairs on its own.

And on day one of the auditions, there was a strong sense of us all making it up as we went along. At first, Ant and I actually sat at the back of the room while auditions were happening. We were given a list of the acts who'd be performing that day and that came in very handy – we used it to cover our faces when we were laughing at some of the singers.

But we quickly realised that us being in the room was unsustainable, not just because we were giggling, but also because it made the acts less likely to confide in us after a performance. So we went outside into the corridor and talked to the acts before and after they performed. Despite that, there was still a sense of something not quite working. For more on this story, we can go over to TV's Simon Cowell . . .

SIMON: 'On the first day we had people coming in, singing and then they left the room. And, as they left the room, we would then talk about them and then they'd come back in and we'd say whether we liked them or not. And after about seven auditions, myself and Pete Waterman went outside and spoke to Ant and Dec and we said, "We're dying on our arses in there." And they said, "Same here." So I said, "I think we should just tell them to their face." Ant and Dec absolutely jumped on that. And I think that was the moment where we really had a connection because all of us understood what was going to make the show work. They were brilliant with the contestants, but, I mean, talk about winging it, that was winging it.'

We actually love winging it, we've always been huge fans of winging anything that's available to be winged.

After the judges started giving the acts their opinions directly, it became more raw and real and it gave me and Dec something much more concrete and immediate to talk to them about.

We would watch the auditions through a crack in the door, as if we were eavesdropping, so we had a sense of the story. And something else happened at those auditions, something that at the time was a first. If a singer got upset or angry after their performance, and wanted to storm off, the camera followed them. Again, it was about being more truthful, taking away the gloss of TV and showing the whole experience, warts and all.

Once all those elements were in place – singers who couldn't sing, alongside singers who could really, really sing and whose lives were transformed by the show – it made for a really fresh and different piece of telly. And, of course, when you added the judges to that, especially a brutally honest

– Will and Gareth always took the time to pose
with enthusiastic fans. –

– Hands up if you've given permission for this
photo to be used in a book. –

– 'Pssst Will. Wanna buy one of these plasmas?' –

Simon Cowell, the show became a smash hit. And, naturally, we like to think we played a part in that too.

> SIMON: 'Ant and Dec have always been very, very funny and very consistent. They do everything with a smile on their face. When it comes to TV, they've got incredible instincts, they just "get it".'

They sound a bit full of themselves to me, these Ant and Dec characters. . .

Being at the auditions also gave us the chance to define our role on the show. We quickly realised it was about encouraging, consoling and congratulating the contestants, and, most crucially of all, taking the mickey out of the judges, especially Simon's rudeness and Pete Waterman's eccentricities.

We did that with a variety of sketches where Ant would play Pete and I would play Simon, complete with high trousers that went up to my nipples. I bet Simon looked forward to seeing those sketches . . .

> SIMON: 'I always dreaded seeing those sketches, waiting to see how Ant and Dec were going to slaughter us every week. But, at the same time, I absolutely loved them. They always made me laugh. I'd bring them back now. I think they should be doing it on *Britain's Got Talent*. I love it when they take the p**s out of us. Me and the boys share a very, very similar sense of humour. We've always had that kind of shorthand.'

Make a note of that: take the p**s out of *BGT* judges more.

And in among all of that, we discovered something that is still a huge part of our TV work today, something we always do on Britain's Got Talent and I'm a Celebrity – try to be the voice of the audience.

The way we see it, it's our job to try to react to what's going on the same way we would if we were sat on the sofa at home. So if someone does something daft, we have a laugh with it; if someone gets upset, we're sympathetic; and if someone chews on a kangaroo testicle, we retch and watch through our fingers.

By the end of the *Pop Idol* auditions, there were two singers who stood out. A kid from Yorkshire who had a stutter, but an incredible singing voice, called Gareth Gates, and the very last person to audition that series, and an act who took the courageous decision of answering back to Simon Cowell: Will Young.

Will answering back to Simon was a big moment. He performed his version of 'Light My Fire', during the second stage of the competition. He got good comments from the first three judges and then it came to Simon, who called it 'average'. Will defended himself and even started to critique Simon's judging – the judge was being judged! People loved it and, strange as it sounds, the general response was, 'Ooh, I didn't know they could answer back.' It really changed the landscape of those act–judge relationships.

Will and Gareth were both really nice lads. They both had very clear ideas of where they wanted their careers to go. Gareth wanted to be the archetypal pop star, which was exactly what Simon Cowell was looking for.

Will, on the other hand, was a bit quirkier, a less 'obvious' pop act, but ultimately won the show, which meant Simon could take them both on – result.

And they were both great guys to work with. Will was more confident, whereas Gareth struggled a bit with his stutter, *but it was fascinating to see them going on such a life-changing journey. In a matter of weeks, they went from anonymity to the whole country – and I really do mean the whole country – talking about them.*

You were either a Will fan or a Gareth fan. Of course, as the hosts, we always remained completely impartial . . . while secretly wanting Will to win. Don't get me wrong, Gareth was a great singer; we were just slightly more drawn to Will because he was a bit different.

And Pop Idol *was a show that completely transformed Dec's and my career, too.*

We got to wear suits for the first time.

Yes, but more importantly, we'd come from Saturday mornings and fart jokes to proper, big grown-up Saturday night telly where millions of people got to know us – 14 million people tuned in to watch that first Pop Idol *final.*

The producers on the show, Nigel Lythgoe, Kenny Warwick and Claire Horton, were brilliant with us two. For a double act who'd never done a show that size, of that importance, they really trusted our instincts. We never felt in any way restricted.

Except when I wore those high trousers to play Simon in the sketches – they made me feel very restricted.

By the time we stood on stage for the final, ready to reveal the winner, the whole country was watching and the electricity in the air that night was something that's hard to match. We've been lucky enough to experience it a few times, with shows like *Britain's Got Talent* and *I'm a Celebrity*, but that first time, the intensity you got from that 'Will or Gareth?' moment, was really something.

Although I have a confession to make.

It was me who got to announce the winner and, when it came to the big moment, I had a mischievous voice in my head that kept saying, 'You COULD say whatever name you like here.' And I hear that voice every time we announce the winner on any of the shows we host. I mean, it would have caused a whole world of trouble if I'd said the winner was Gareth, not Will, but I could have done it, couldn't I?

Thank God you didn't or we'd have been sacked on the spot.

The second series in 2003 was just as big too, and – for us – was memorable for two things: firstly, the winner, Michelle McManus, who was an amazing singer and different from a 'conventional' pop star, and, secondly, the TV crime of the century.

As part of the Pop Idol set, there were loads of giant plasma screens on the studio floor and, the day after the final, the studio was being emptied, or 'de-rigged', to use the technical term. Two blokes arrived and told the studio receptionist they were 'here to take the plasmas'. She directed them to the studio, where they proceeded to remove all the TVs, load them into their waiting van and take them away. So far, so normal.

Then, three hours later, two blokes arrived and told the studio receptionist they were 'here to take the plasmas'. You're ahead of me, aren't you? The first two were just a couple of blokes with a van and a lot of bottle.

Can you imagine? Two blokes had basically conned a load of people into believing they belonged in a TV studio and knew what they were doing – and then they ended up making a good few quid from nothing more than bravado.

In many ways, they were the Ant and Dec of plasma TV theft.

Pop Idol series 2 final. Ant forgot his suit. –

p Idol crew mark 2 revel in the glamour
f a red hotel function room carpet. –

– If you're thinking
'whatever happened to
Chris Hyde, the guy who
came fourth in series 2 of
Pop Idol?' – he tried to
take that cuddly toy off
Dec, that's what. –

– Dec as Simon. Unnerving. –

BRIT
ARDS
5
with
MasterCard
co.uk
#BRITs2015
BRIT
AWARDS
2015

5

THE BRITS AND SOME OTHER BITS

Disclaimer: This is the pick 'n' mix chapter of the book, which is another way of saying that this is where we've put all the stories that don't fit anywhere else.

And we start by briefly flashing back to 1995 and the PJ & Duncan years.

Do we have to? I've only just recovered from the trauma of chapter 2.

And, specifically, that year's BRITs, where a certain 19-year-old duo were sat in Alexandra Palace, waiting with bated breath as The Kinks' Ray Davies took to the stage to announce the nominations for Best Newcomer.

I'm getting nervous all over again . . .

Over to you, Ray.

'The nominees are:
Echobelly
Eternal
Oasis
PJ & Duncan
Portishead
And the winner is . . .'

Fingers crossed . . .

'Oasis.'

Oh.

Yes, that's right, we didn't win, but PJ & Duncan were nevertheless nominated as Best Newcomer at the BRITs. If it was possible for a book to hear a reader laughing, that would be happening right now, wouldn't it?

Being beaten by Oasis made for a disappointing night, not just because we lost, but also because our record company had persuaded us to 'make an entrance' by turning up to the ceremony in an ice-cream van.

Unsurprisingly, it was a complete disaster. The two of us were packed into the van, crammed against boxes of cones and the handle of the Mr Whippy machine, as we crawled through traffic on the way to Alexandra Palace. In the end, we arrived so late that everyone had gone inside and the red carpet was being rolled up. Our 'ker-azy' stunt had embarrassingly backfired.

Much like the old ice-cream van we'd been sat in for two hours. But let's leave the 1995 fiasco there and jump forward six whole years to these words:

'Welcome to the BRITs 2001. We're your hosts, Ant and Dec.'

ITV chose us to host the biggest night in the British music calendar because we were riding high with *sm:tv* and *cd:uk* and, more importantly, because everyone else was too busy or too expensive.

By this point, we had just signed an exclusive deal with ITV and it was an enormous thrill to be hosting such a big event and something we'd grown up watching. The BRITs are always held in a huge, glamorous venue (Alexandra Palace, Earls Court or the O2) and there are thousands of people there, including the crème de la crème *of the British music scene. It's a night full of glitz, glamour and excitement.*

People walk around the arena, chatting to each other and pouring wine – it sometimes feels like an enormous restaurant where all the customers are famous people. It's the most fun party to be a guest at. But it's a tough gig if you're the hosts.

We knew it wasn't going well when someone came up to us and ordered two bottles of rioja and a gin and tonic.

The thing about the BRITs is that you've got two different audiences – an arena full of music industry people who couldn't care less what you're saying, and then there's the viewers at home. We decided to largely disregard the music industry bods and focus on the people watching on telly, but we still found it a really tough night.

If we're honest, it shook us a bit. It was the biggest hosting gig we'd taken on at that time and, even though people had warned us that the hosts can find it tough, we had no idea on what scale until we did it.

On the plus side, we got to meet loads of amazing performers and award presenters. It was the first time we met a little band you may have heard of called Coldplay. They were making their BRITs debut and they told me and Ant that they were excited to meet us because they were fans of *sm:tv*, which we were incredibly chuffed about. We still catch up with the guys whenever we can and have seen them perform in Australia, America and even joined them on stage in Newcastle, when they did a benefit gig for the homeless charity Crisis at our old haunt, the Tyne Theatre & Opera House. They always invite us to go backstage and see them, which is very kind. We absolutely love those guys and think they're so, so talented.

In a completely unconnected sentence, we hope they continue to give us free tickets to their shows.

Long story short, though, it was a long, difficult night and, ultimately, we didn't have a nice time hosting the BRITs in 2001. We came off stage saying, 'We are never, ever doing that again.'

Anyway, let's move on, what's next?

'Welcome to the BRITs 2015. We're your hosts, Ant and Dec.'

What can we say? Fourteen years is a long time in showbusiness . . .

We were on holiday together in Dubai when we got a call from the organisers asking if we were interested in having another go at hosting. Our first response was, 'No way, absolutely not, never gonna happen, no thank you, next question please–'

We get the picture. It was a no.

Our manager said, 'They've asked if you'll at least meet them?' And we started talking it over, wondering if it had been as bad as we remembered. After all, the person who ordered the rioja and gin and tonic had been a very good tipper. Before we knew it, we'd agreed to sit down with the BRITs team.

The chairman of the BRITs that year was a guy called Max Lousada, who was also the CEO of Warner Music. We chatted with him and were so impressed by how enthusiastic he was about the show. He said he wanted to make it the best BRITs ever. The British music scene was going through a brilliant period, and lots of big acts had already confirmed, including a very special headliner. Madonna was going to be performing at the ceremony for the first time in 20 years and we were the only hosts he wanted. By the end of the meeting, we heard ourselves saying, 'We're in!'

And Max wasn't wrong; it really was a brilliant time for British music. Adele had become a superstar, our old mates Coldplay were now ginormous, there was Sam Smith, Paloma Faith, Ed Sheeran – it was a golden era for them all and Madonna headlining? What a brilliant ending that would be . . .

Yes, quite.

Max said we could have the freedom to do it our way and have fun with it. We also knew from experience that we would be making the show for the people at home – this time we were completely ready for the giant restaurant where no one listens and it didn't bother us one jot, not even when someone asked us for a bottle of sauvignon blanc and two mojitos.

On the night, we had an idea of something we could do with Kim Kardashian, who was there with her husband Kanye West and had agreed to present one of the awards. We didn't tell her about it beforehand because we knew one of her entourage would have vetoed it, as so often happens at things like this . . .

Can I just say that 'One of her entourage would have vetoed it' is arguably the most showbiz sentence I've ever heard you say.

Thank you, darling.
   The idea was that we'd have a bit of fun with her when she came out on stage, saying something along the lines of, 'Can we have a picture?', and then when she inevitably said yes, we'd hand her Dec's phone and get her to take a picture of us two.

Just brilliant. No other word for it.

She was one of the most famous women on the planet and we were getting her to take a photo of two lads from Newcastle.

Yes, yes, we get it. Jokes are never funny when you explain them, as Ant has just proved.

Kim came out to present the award and we absolutely nailed the set-up and asked her for a photo. 'Sure,' she said. Bingo! Now for the killer punchline. 'This'll slay 'em,' I thought. But before we could smash that punchline out of the park, she leant over and took Dec's phone out of his sweaty, excited hand. She turned around, got all three of us in the shot and took a selfie. Joke knackered in one swoop of Kim K's delicately manicured hand.

And, even worse, my phone decided to freeze at that exact moment, so now there's a photo of us two taking a selfie with Kim Kardashian but the selfie itself doesn't actually exist.

- Despite our endorsement, Coldplay's range of bracelets never really took off. -

- 'Welcome to the BRITs 2015 . . . I can already see a lady in a black dress and a bald man talking over us.' -

- The selfie that never was with Kim Kardashian. -

Plus, it just looked like Dec really wanted a selfie with Kim Kardashian and he couldn't wait till after the BRITs to ask her! So unprofessional. But the big story of that year at the BRITs was Madonna.

Oh Madonna, Madonna, Madonna.

There was huge excitement and expectation about her closing the show. As we delivered our last link – into her performance – we felt like we'd sailed the good ship BRITs safely into the harbour without any major incidents.

How wrong we were.

Ed Sheeran had just been presented with Best British Album and then we said, 'Ladies and gentlemen, Madonna!'

As her performance started, we took out our earpieces and high-fived, congratulating each other on hosting a BRITs without a single hitch. We were handed a glass of champagne; we toasted each other's professionalism, boogied our way out of the arena and made our way back to our dressing room.

Unbeknownst to us, as we were walking back to the dressing room, Madonna had a now famous wardrobe malfunction with her cape and took a spectacular fall backwards down a flight of stairs. In the space of three seconds (and about five steps), she accidentally created the most memorable BRITs moment of the last decade. Meanwhile, the two of us were blissfully ignorant of the Queen of Pop tumble down the stairs and, after a long walk through the O2 and its labyrinthine corridors, we arrived back in our dressing room, where the TV was on and the Ten O'Clock News was just starting:

'Tonight's top story: Chaos at the BRITs as Madonna takes dramatic fall.'

We nearly dropped our champagne. What were they talking about? We hadn't seen any chaos and we hosted the bloody thing. We watched the full story open-mouthed. After spending a couple of minutes making sure everyone was OK and discussing how sorry we felt for Madonna, we turned to each other and both said exactly the same thing: 'Looks like we've got a sketch for Takeaway on Saturday!'

(And, don't worry, the *Saturday Night Takeaway* chapter is coming soon, dear reader.)

We hosted the BRITs again the following year, but no one fell down any stairs and, that year, the whole ceremony really did pass off without incident. We were almost disappointed.

Of course, the BRITs aren't the only awards we've had an ongoing relationship with – we have flirted with other ceremonies behind their back. The main one being the National Television Awards, where we've been lucky enough to do quite well down the years.

But one of our favourite ever NTA moments isn't an award we won, but a performance we did with the late, great Sir Bruce Forsyth in 2012. When we got the call, it was a complete no-brainer – Sir Bruce was a showbiz legend and someone we'd always looked up to.

To be fair, we both look up to most people.

od these are heavy, just keep smiling. –

– That time our mams won at the NTAs. –

– Number 13 – the icing
on the cake. –

Bruce insisted we did plenty of rehearsal, which suited us, because we got to spend plenty of time with a total legend of showbusiness. So that January, a few weeks before the ceremony, the three of us met up at a golf club in west London called Dukes Meadows to practise the routine.

It had to be a golf club with Sir Bruce, obviously.

We were performing a version of 'Let There Be Love' and, after rehearsals, we all sat down for a cup of tea and he regaled us with stories–

Excellent use of 'regaled'.

Thanks.
He regaled us with stories of working with everybody from Morecambe and Wise to Sammy Davis Jr and we were just transfixed. He was really lovely to us and very complimentary about what we do, which we were both blown away by. He was a real gentleman; we absolutely loved him and adored working with him.

When our eyes met across a crowded pretend youth club back in 1990, we never dreamt that, one day, we'd sit around with a cup of tea and a biscuit casually talking to a legend like Sir Bruce Forsyth about showbusiness.

When it came to the day of the NTAs, we rehearsed again, this time on stage at the O2 in Greenwich. We turned up at the venue on a very cold January morning. It was absolutely freezing and Sir Bruce was already up on stage marking through his routine like a true pro, wrapped up in his overcoat and a big scarf.

We got up on stage and started rehearsing with him. We were all wearing layers trying to keep warm, but it was so cold inside the arena that morning. Then we noticed that Sir Bruce had a tiny little dewdrop on the end of his nose (understandable given the temperature) . . .

. . . but he didn't seem to have noticed it (understandable given that he was in the middle of a huge song and dance routine).

So, we had the same thought everyone has when someone you're with has a little dribble on their nose, or something on their face. Do we say something? Or is it rude? We should probably just leave it.

We thought, 'Let's just get on with rehearsal then we can deal with it afterwards.' Halfway through the routine we came to the section where Sir Bruce got in between the two of us and said, 'The last time
I did something like this was with the Muppets.'
   And he pronounced the 'p's in Muppets with such an enthusiastic nod of his head that the dewdrop flew off the end of his nose and landed . . .

Right onto my bottom lip.
   I don't mind telling you, dear reader, I froze. I didn't know what to do. I didn't want to wipe it off straight away, in case I caused offence, but I needed to deal with the situation. I gently stuck out my bottom lip like a sulky toddler and carried on with the routine, but much like trying to eat a doughnut without licking your lips, when you're not allowed to do something, you become obsessed with it. I managed to carry on and by the end of the routine, well, it had pretty much been absorbed into my system.

– All hail Sir Bruce
Of Forsyth. –

– And what do putts make? Tiny prizes. –

And the great news is that Dec now shares some of Sir Bruce's DNA.

I do not share any DNA with Sir Bruce Forsyth.

Well, you do love tap-dancing and you plan to work until your eighties, that's my point.

And what do points make? Prizes!
    Oh my God you're right . . .
Shortly after the NTAs incident, we got a call from Vernon Kay, who was friendly with Sir Bruce. Vernon said, 'The Don wants to play golf with you.'

'The Don' is what Vernon called Sir Bruce. I want to make it clear that Ant and I have no connections with organised crime.

Sir Bruce was a member of the world-famous Wentworth Golf Club and it was so nice to see him again.

To see him nice.
    Gah! There it is again.

When we turned up to meet him at the clubhouse, he didn't disappoint, he was in full Brucie mode. He hosted the game of golf like it was a TV show. He said, 'Right, we're playing a new format; we'll change partners every six holes and first up I'm playing with Ant, Dec you start with Vernon. Is everybody ready? Good luck, let's go.' We played three different formats within the round of golf and Sir Bruce won them all. It was such a good game.

Good game, good game.
  I can't stop it . . .

At one point, Dec made a birdie, which, if you're not a golf fan, is a good score, and meant he received the honour of hitting the first shot on the next hole. He stepped up and royally scuffed it straight into the bushes. Sir Bruce cried out, 'Oh no! It's a FUAB!'

Clocking our quizzical looks, Sir Bruce explained that a FUAB is a 'f**k-up after a birdie!'

After the game, we were invited back to The Don's house for a bite to eat and our trophy presentation. He gave us a tour of the place and we were introduced to his housekeeper, a lovely Filipino lady, who brought us some delicious homemade spring rolls, which Sir Bruce always liked after a round of golf. The moment she saw me and Dec she screamed, 'Oh my God! It's you two! My favourites! You two are my favourites on TV!'

Quick as a flash, Sir Bruce jumped in and said, 'Oi! You said I was your favourite!'

We had to leave before we'd had a chance to tuck into our food because we were already running late for something else, so Sir Bruce went off and got some kitchen foil out, wrapped up our spring rolls and sent us off with a little packed lunch. What a man.

We promised him a rematch at our golf club. Sadly, we never got to play another round with The Don before he passed away, but it was always the most enormous privilege to spend time with him.

And talking of legends on golf courses, that reminds me of that time we were with Alan Shearer . . .

From the BRITs to the NTAs to golf and spring rolls with Sir Bruce to Alan Shearer. Told you it was the pick 'n' mix chapter.

We should first make it clear to anyone who might not know – Alan Shearer is the very definition of the word 'legend' to any Newcastle United fan, including us two.

Hanging out with Alan started with an invitation from golf champion Lee Westwood to be his guests at the Masters Tournament in Augusta, Georgia, in 2012. It's like being asked to play a round with Sir Bruce Forsyth – you don't turn down those kinds of opportunities.

Off we flew. When we got off the plane and switched on our phones, up pinged a message from Lee, saying, 'I hope you're ready to work.' I thought, 'What does that mean?'

I thought, 'I haven't switched off my data roaming, that message probably just cost me a tenner.'

Anyway, he explained that as part of the Par 3 – which is a mini competition the day before the real Masters Tournament starts – I was going to be caddying for him and Dec was going to be caddying for Thomas Bjorn (who would go on to captain the European Ryder Cup team in 2018).

It was an amazing opportunity; we felt like competition winners and we had a brilliant time doing it. But let's get back to Alan Shearer before this chapter goes even more off course.

Nice golf pun.

Was it? Oh yeah . . .

Alan Shearer was also at the Masters with a load of guys we know from Newcastle and we all ended up staying in the same row of houses in what became christened 'Geordie Close'.

After a long flight, we arrived at the house, knackered and ready for an early night so we could be on top form for caddying duties the next morning. And no sooner had we got there than Mr Shearer pops over from across the road. He'd arrived earlier than us and was full of beans, asking how we were and what we thought of the house. And then he said, 'Oh, by the way, I've got your kettle.'

We looked confused so the former England captain explained: he'd got the keys and looked round all the available houses and done what we would probably all do – picked the best one for him and his mates. One tiny detail escaped him, though; his house, the 'best' house, didn't have a kettle. Alan thought he would remedy this by letting himself into the house we were going to be staying in and pinching ours.

We told him that was very unfair, and that we would very much like our kettle back. Then we remembered we were talking to Alan Shearer and there was absolutely no chance that was going to happen, so I decided to go for the next best thing. I said to Newcastle United's all-time leading goalscorer that I wanted a cup of tea in the morning.

'Tough,' said the man who's also scored the most goals in the history of the Premier League. 'I've got your kettle.'

'You're very good at golf, high five!' -

- 'Guys, this fist bump has really
overshadowed my high five.' -

- Finally a golf club in
Dec's size. -

For some reason, Dec wasn't prepared to be on the losing side of this one without a fight. He went in with both feet and told the 1995 Premier League winner if he wasn't bringing back our kettle, he could bring us both hot drinks at 8am sharp the next morning. And I thought, 'Go on, Dec, tell Newcastle's finest-ever number 9 what to do.'

Obviously, I never thought for a moment that a man who scored 16 career hat-tricks would do it, but I was enjoying the tussle.

That night, we went out with the sheet metal worker's son and the rest of the lads (so much for the early night . . .) and we got on to the subject of timekeeping.

I told the man who was once the most expensive footballer on the planet that Dec was always late – wherever we went, he was 15 minutes late. The scorer of 30 goals in 63 games for England was not impressed. He is a stickler for punctuality and believes that, 'To be early is to be on time, to be on time is to be late and to be late is not acceptable.' And that is a direct quote.

The following morning, I was woken from my slumber by a banging on the front door followed by the sound of someone who already had a set of keys letting themselves in. The next thing I heard was the intruder stomping up the stairs with their dulcet Geordie tones belting out 'Oh What A Beautiful Morning' . . .

*My bedroom door burst open and in walked the 1995 PFA Player of the Year holding two mugs. He laid a coffee down on my bedside table, threw back my duvet and shouted, 'Get up, you lazy b*****d!' Then he headed for Dec's room.*

He burst into mine like he was through on goal with only the keeper to beat. He slammed the milky tea down on my bedside table and leant down towards my face.

'Happy now?' he asked.

I rolled over, looked at the bedside clock, which read 8.01. I couldn't believe my luck. I turned back to the ever-punctual Alan and said . . .

'You're late.'

Back of the net.

And that's where we're ending the chapter, is it? With you getting one over on Alan Shearer?

Yes. Yes, we are.

6

SATURDAY NIGHT TAKEAWAY

'*Saturday Night Takeaway* makes other TV shows look like they're not even trying.' — Rob Brydon, March 2020 (after he'd just been on *Saturday Night Takeaway*)

Thank you, Rob, we'll pay you the next time we see you.

Saturday Night Takeaway is without a shadow of a doubt the busiest, craziest, most complicated thing we've ever done, but before we tell you any more about that, I think we should hear from the people who are the most important part of it all – our audience.

In the early days of the show, a researcher would ask some of the audience to tell us a funny fact about themselves. Below are a few of our favourites we found when we were going through the archives for this book:

'I have three nipples and I often show them off to customers in the pub I work in.'

'I thought the cat was sunbathing in the garden for the day. But he was dead.'

'My face is badly disfigured from when I was severely burnt. I have no eyebrows and I can make funny faces.'

'I was in a car with my friends when I really needed to go to the toilet – so I had a s**t in a plastic bag.'

'My wife says I blink a lot.'

'My daughter gets head lice quite often and I enjoy bursting them – they make a popping noise.'

'While queuing for the cash machine, my nipple shields fell out.'

'I once ate only breakfast cereal for a month. I was rushed to hospital and had to have my gall bladder removed.'

'I have three nipples – at school they called me Triple Nipple.'

God, I love our audience.

But now we've given you a flavour of them, let's explain how we came to make a show that triple-nippled people want to be a part of.

It started in 2002 and was the show we always wanted to make – we grew up adoring programmes like Noel's House Party and Game for a Laugh, alongside more recent TV shows like Don't Forget Your Toothbrush. What all three of those programmes have in common is that they were 'multi-item' shows. They weren't just about one style of TV; they would include pranks, sketches, games, quizzes – they had an 'anything goes' attitude. And we thought – and hoped – there could be room for something like that fronted by a cheeky Geordie duo.

It also helped that, after *Pop Idol*, a primetime audience actually knew who we were. I mean, they didn't know which one was Ant and which one was Dec, but they recognised our faces and voices and that was at least a start.

At the beginning, the unique selling point of the show was a member of the audience could win the contents of the ad breaks – it was a brilliantly simple idea and, even better, one that the BBC couldn't do. And after putting the show together with a crack creative team at Granada Television, including Duncan Gray, Nigel Hall, Leon Wilde, Chris Power (who's still our director) and Siobhan Greene (who's still part of Team Takeaway today), we went on air on 18th June 2002.

The idea was always that *Takeaway* would be a weekly event where we could do <u>anything</u>. We've always approached each individual section of the show as if it were a programme in its own right. Whether that's an audience surprise, a hidden-camera stunt, a musical performance, Ant versus Dec, a sketch or any of the other hundreds of things we've done down the years. They each have their own dedicated production team –

and we all put as much time, effort and resources into each of them as we would if they were all shows of their own.

It's a beast, is what we're trying to say, a 90-minute rollercoaster ride of live TV where everyone flies by the seat of their pants.

And who doesn't love sitting on the seat of their pants in a rollercoaster that's also a beast?

From 2002, the show ran for nine series and we had more fun than anyone should legally be allowed to have on television. Highlights included both incarnations of Little Ant and Dec (who would interview A-list stars and ask them questions no one else could get away with), giving away prizes worth hundreds of thousands of pounds, and inviting on incredible guests like Mariah Carey, George Clooney, Will Smith and Beyoncé.

I remember two things about having Beyoncé on the show. Firstly, we did a sketch where she ate a pork pie (random) and, secondly, she had the biggest entourage I've ever seen. When she arrived at the studio, I was asked to 'clear the corridor' by her security team. I thought, 'Hang on, it's our show, this is our corridor'. . . as I obediently cleared the corridor by diving into the nearest toilets.

One of my fondest memories was going to America for an Undercover on Simon Cowell, where we auditioned for American Idol . . .

> SIMON COWELL: 'I can remember it like it was yesterday. We were in Texas and it was one of those days where every singer was terrible, and Ant and Dec genuinely fooled me.
>
> They're so good at that and it was a risk, because it must have cost a fortune. If I'd recognised them, the whole thing would have been a complete waste of time, but I thought it was

– Original Little Ant and Dec,
new Little Ant and Dec and actual
Ant and Dec (also quite little). –

– Secret filming while
disguised as a chair and
a table (don't ask). –

hilarious. I actually went on the show to see me judging them and it was really, really funny.'

They're the nicest audition comments I've ever seen him give.

Then, in 2009, after nine series, we rested the show for four years. It was time for the rollercoaster that's also a beast to stand down for a while.

Usually, in telly, when someone says a show is being 'rested', it means 'cancelled', but Takeaway genuinely needed a rest, it was knackered – who wouldn't be exhausted after going at it every Saturday night for an hour and a half for nine years?

You might want to rephrase that . . .

We felt like we were running out of ideas and the last thing we wanted was for the show to end up like the wholemeal loaf that's currently in my bread bin: stale.

Is that loaf still there? It was on the turn when I came to yours last week.

One of the reasons for that is that *Takeaway* is the show with our names on the door, so to speak. With *I'm a Celebrity* and *Britain's Got Talent* (both of which we absolutely LOVE doing), we're a big part of the show, but they are formats about people with an incredible talent . . . or people who like munching on crocodile penis . . . whereas we're at the centre of every single thing that happens on *Takeaway*. It's our baby and it means the world to us.

While it had a little nap, we hosted other shows, like Red or Black? *(where contestants could win a million pounds on one spin of a roulette wheel) and* Push the Button *(a game show where two families went head to head across various challenges), but we kept having ideas for Saturday Night Takeaway. That's the thing about Takeaway; its strength has always been that it can accommodate endless new ideas, a show where we can really push the boundaries creatively – that's what excites us the most.*

That was a big part of why, in 2013, we decided to bring it back. And, of course, if you're bringing something back, it's the law of telly that it has to be 'bigger and better than ever'.

I mean, there was no chance of us two getting any bigger, that ship's sailed, but the show could get bigger.

We did that with an amazing new production team that included some of the most talented people in telly: Siobhan Greene, Richard Cowles, Chris Power, Pete Ogden, Saul Fearnley, Diego Rincón, Gemma Nightingale, Becca Walker, Marcus McKinlay, Paula Cowles, Sophie Bowdery and the writers Andy Milligan, Mark Busk-Cowley and the Dawson Brothers.

Once we'd got them recruited (in exchange for getting mentioned in a book) we were determined to make sure we had loads of new content and lots of big names. Across that first series back then we had people like Lewis Hamilton, Ricky Gervais and David Walliams (who were guest announcers); Sir Bruce Forsyth, Mila Kunis, Gerard Butler (who got the Little Ant and Dec treatment); and Simon Cowell, Robbie Williams and Michael Bublé (who all took part in The End of the Show Show).

ROBBIE WILLIAMS: 'Takeaway is completely unlike any other show I do. It's all about silliness. But it's Olympic level silliness. As light entertainers, Ant and Dec are Olympians. The energy they create is magical, which is why I feel so comfortable on that show. If something goes wrong, it's embraced. It becomes part of the show. For me, a lot of things that I do are like work and when I'm on Takeaway, it's not work.'

Did you hear that? We're Olympians! Olympians for whom things often go wrong and who don't have any actual medals, but Olympians nonetheless.

DAVID WALLIAMS: 'They're very generous when you

go on *Takeaway*. They don't mind you getting a laugh, you know? Some performers look aghast if someone else gets a laugh on their show, but they're not like that at all. When they invite you on the show, they want you to be yourself and do your thing; there isn't an ounce of them that wants to take the laughs from you.'

I'm just happy if anyone gets a laugh on *Takeaway*, us two don't manage it very often. . .

We also had bags of new ideas: the Supercomputer (a giant computer that toured the nation's shopping centres giving away holidays), the aforementioned End of the Show Show (a huge show-stopping performance that closed every show), seven brand-new audience surprises (where we, er, surprise members of the audience), I'm a Celebrity . . . Get Out of Me Ear! (a brand-new hidden-camera feature), and we also had one of the biggest and scariest things we've ever done – going Undercover on The Jeremy Kyle Show . . . in New York. The first thing you should know about this whole Undercover shoot is that it took years of planning and was very, very expensive.

Or, as I like to say, vey, vey expensive.

And that meant that, to use a technical TV term, it was really important we didn't balls it up. We chose to 'hit' Jeremy in America for several reasons: it was bigger and bolder, but also because he would be off his guard – he would never expect us to fly to New York to stitch him up. All sounds pretty easy, right?

Wrong.

The first problem was Jeremy's and our schedules. We worked out that the only time his show was recording when we were available was the middle of December, straight after I'm a Celebrity. That meant we did a 24-hour flight back from Australia, got back to London, packed another bag and then flew to New York. By the time we arrived in the City That Never Sleeps, we had the most horrendous jet lag imaginable. And, when you added that to the stress of a very expensive and tricky-to-pull-off shoot, well, let's just say the city wasn't the only thing that didn't sleep when we were in New York.

I still remember the nerves on the day of filming. We hadn't done an Undercover for almost five years and it was terrifying. The idea we'd come up with was that I would be appearing as a contributor on his US show. I would be posing as Mike, a man whose wife Janine was distressed at her husband's addiction to plastic surgery. And no wonder poor Janine was distressed, because Mike had had plastic surgery to look like his dead cat Smudge.

It sounds silly when you write it all out, doesn't it?

Yeah, funny that.

While I was cast as ol' cat-face Mike, Ant would be playing a 'safety supervisor' called Howard, who appeared later in the story. On the day of the shoot, I had to get to make-up at 4am and, right from the get-go, there was one thought endlessly running around my brain: 'I'm about to go on *The Jeremy Kyle Show* USA pretending to be a cat. A cat with an American accent.'

That's the other thing about when we do Undercovers in America, we invariably have to pretend to be American (we're clever like that . . .) and that means we have to train with a dialect coach to get the accent right. I mean, whatever I'm trained to do, I always sound a bit Geordie, but the pressure was really on Dec for this one.

I'm sweating all over again just thinking about it.

The other thing I hadn't really considered was that I would have to do everything a real contributor on the show does. We'd set the whole thing up through Jeremy's producer, but he was one of the only members of the team who knew what was going on. And, in order to make it look as authentic as possible, I would have to turn up at the studios, spend time with my fellow guests and answer questions from a researcher who had no idea what we had planned.

At least when we'd gone Undercover on Simon Cowell on American Idol, we had each other, but this time Dec was all on his own.

And, I really can't stress this enough, I had the face of a cat.

Although the great thing about the guy we'd created was that he had gone too far with plastic surgery, so if the prosthetics looked a bit weird, as they often can, then it didn't matter.

It came to the big moment and I was hidden away in the gallery with our team. Just before the show started recording, Jeremy came out to say hello to the audience. He explained he had a great show for them, including one guy who'd had plastic surgery to look like his cat.

I was sat backstage, chatting to a woman from Minnesota who'd married a car or something, thinking, 'God, that's me.' Then I heard Jeremy finishing his opening speech and he asked the audience if they were ready, they screamed 'Yes!' and he shouted, 'Then let's get ready to ruuuuumble!'

I immediately thought, 'He knows! S**t! He knows! He bloody *knows! This is the most expensive Undercover we've ever done, and he's sussed it before we've even started.'*

I was thinking exactly the same.

But with the face of a cat.

Then Jeremy introduced me to the studio audience, and I walked out, shaking like a leaf. As we'd planned, I got down on all fours and brushed up against the legs of the actress we'd hired to play Janine. Jeremy started asking me questions and I realised, 'Oh my God, he doesn't know, he's going with it!'

'Let's get ready to rumble' was just something he said to his audience.

Then I could relax . . . and concentrate on telling the story of how I used a litter tray, caught mice and ate cat food.

Actually, maybe 'relax' isn't the right word . . .

I was still in the studio gallery thinking, 'We're in! He's got no idea! We haven't ballsed it up!' My part of the sting was still to come, but for a few enjoyable minutes I got to sit back and watch Dec deliver one of the finest performances of his illustrious acting career.

When we're doing any of these Undercovers, once you get past that initial terror of them (let's get ready to) rumbling it in the first few minutes, your mindset shifts to just trying to remember as many of the lines and ideas you've prepared and getting as much comedy as you possibly can out of the situation. I thought, 'If he asks me this, I can shift my answer towards the idea that I poo in a litter tray, or that I'm carrying my dead cat's ashes everywhere I go' – that kind of thing.

A quick reminder that this is our actual job . . .

Once I'd managed to go through every last crazy statement I could remember, it was time for Howard Newman, Chief Health and Safety Officer for the Tri-state Area, to come in.

- Brits abroad. -

Our alter-egos: Howard the safety supervisor and Mike the human cat.

- In LA for the Gordon Ramsay Undercover: 'It's going to wind him up *this* much'. -

- Yes, those are fangs. -

He looked quite like Ant McPartlin, that Howard Newman bloke. Very handsome.

I walked into the studio, accompanied by an extra carrying a giant net, explaining that I had to shut the studio down due to a 'big cat' being on the loose. Jeremy still didn't know what was going on at this point – and that's when we revealed all.

And he was furious – he threw a chair across the studio floor and screamed 'Nooo!'

You have full permission to stop reading the book right now and watch it on YouTube, it's a proper laugh.

It was one of the best Undercovers we'd ever done. And, that night, we went to see the Rolling Stones in New York, then the evening finished with us two, in a bar in Greenwich Village, sharing a drink with Jeremy.

Obviously, I kept the cat prosthetics on, just to rub his nose in it.

The other big American Undercovers we've done in the last few years are Gordon Ramsay and James Corden. With Gordon, we posed as a father- and-son building maintenance team, and, after endlessly interrupting filming, we 'accidentally' locked him in his dressing room while he was shooting the American version of MasterChef – Dec sat on his toilet (complete with 'stomach upset'), while I put an axe through the door.

With Gordon, we really wanted to push him to the point where he lost it and started swearing at us and he certainly didn't disappoint. He was so angry, I actually thought he was going to punch me at one point.

I was all right, I had an axe.

But once he calmed down and realised all the effort we'd gone to, like a lot of the people we do an Undercover on he saw that, in a weird way, it's a compliment that we'd go to that much trouble for him.

And whenever we've been to any of his restaurants since, we always get very well looked after.

Although I always take my axe with me, just to be on the safe side.

James Corden was also great fun to 'get'. We gave him a day from hell at the studios for *The Late Late Show*. We made him late for work, we stole his parking space and then we took part in a Mr and Mrs-style feature on his show called 'Face Your Fiancé'. Us two played the boyfriends of two women (they were actresses) who answered questions about their relationship over Skype. By the end of it, James thought Ant's character had fallen through a glass coffee table and had a bookcase land on top of him. It looked as if he had been seriously injured in the middle of James's show. Poor Mr Corden was in pieces.

Much like that coffee table . . .

James was like a lot of people, in that once we'd revealed it was us, he slowly began piecing together all the weird stuff that had happened that day and how he'd reacted to it – it's like waking up after a dream for them, they're all thinking, 'Did that really happen? Am I remembering that right?'

When we set up Jamie Oliver, he was texting us for days afterwards about stuff that kept coming back to him.
    But Undercover wasn't the only bit of hidden-camera high jinks we got up to when the show came back. One of the other new features was a stunt where celebs wore an earpiece and had to do everything we told them to – or, as it's otherwise known, I'm a Celebrity . . .

All together now . . .

Get Out of Me Eeeeeeeeaaaaarrrrr!

Get Out of Me Eeeeeeeeaaaaarrrrr!

We did a little pilot for it, just to test out the idea, and we chose Louis Walsh to be our first celeb. It turned out to be one of the best decisions we've ever made. Louis was incredible – he did absolutely everything we said. The set-up was that he was 'interviewing' new builders and we had him wearing a crown as the king of pop, showing off a shrine to himself and, most memorably of all, phoning Dannii Minogue . . . with a banana.

I laughed so much that the back of my head was hurting by the end of it.

What was supposed to be the pilot became one of the funniest parts of the new series. To this day, every time I see Louis in person or on TV, there are two words that spring to mind:

X Factor.

No, banana phone.

Oh yeah, that makes more sense.
After that first shoot, we knew we had something special, something new and, most importantly, something where we didn't have to pretend to be cats. Over the last few years, we've been lucky enough to do it with Peter Crouch and Abbey Clancy, Cheryl, Dermot O'Leary, Anthony Joshua and Richard Madeley.

Again, you might want to rephrase that.
It's so much fun to do, not just because we get to spend a day laughing our heads off, but also because it uses one of the skills we've learnt from doing years and years of live telly – reacting

149

quickly and in the moment. For us, it's a kind of improvisation and so much of it is reactive and made up on the spot, which is one of the ways we love to work.

So those improvisational theatre games from your first day on ***Byker Grove*** **came in handy in the end?**

Perhaps. But I still cringe thinking about them 30 years later.

When I said at the start of this book that Ant loves to push things, this is a great example of that – he LOVES doing these so much. Dermot's probably sums that up best. We did it in the middle of a supermarket and it was the first time we'd done a Get Out of Me Ear out and about with the public. Ant was in his element suggesting stuff for Dermot to do.

What can I say? I just love supermarkets.
   The minute we'd finished filming that one, Dermot came into the little control room we had, and after hours of obeying our every whim, he told Dec he was 'awful' but that I was the 'absolute worst'. He told me that at one point I'd asked him to pick up a baby out of its pram. He quite rightly refused, but I'd completely forgotten I'd even said it.

Talking of babies, as we mentioned earlier, ***Takeaway*** **is our baby and, like all babies, it needs constant attention. That means we're working on it all the year round. Whether that's planning a big Undercover shoot (which can take years), working out where the series finale will come from or having ideas for audience surprises, it's the show that never, ever stops.**

> DAVID: "They work incredibly hard, especially on *Takeaway*. I don't think people necessarily see that, but that show takes up so much of their time. And people might not immediately realise, but they are both super-smart. They are incredibly switched on

- *Takeaway On Tour*. Spoiler alert: Neither of us can play the guitar. -

- Script meeting with producer Gemma . . .
  who brought her own sofa. -

- Rocky and Hurley on
tour with us - finally,
a decent double act in
this book. -

and knowledgeable about TV and they've got great takes and
theories about stuff.

They're not like some pretty face just saying something from an
autocue. They're both naturally very good at coming up with
stuff off the cuff, because so much of what they do is live TV –
they're never out of their depth with anything that's going on.

They're completely engaged in every single aspect of the show and
they do everything they can to make every single moment work.'

*That is so lovely . . . although did he say we haven't got
pretty faces?*

He's got a point.
     **Being in the moment is so important when you're hosting a
show like *Takeaway* though. Occasionally, you have a moment
where, in the middle of all the madness, you think to yourself,
'I'm hosting a live TV show.' Your brain kind of steps outside of
what you're doing, and you can detach a bit and think, 'This
is exciting' or, 'I didn't expect that' or even, 'People at home
are going to love that!' You can become an observer and a
participant at the same time.**

*And with the kind of shows we do, the fact they're watched by
families means that when you do an audience surprise and see
people sat on their sofa, having a drink and some food on a
Saturday night, you think, 'That's our audience, that's how they
watch the show', and that's a real buzz. It gives you a real sense
of what people are doing while they're watching you.*

SIMON: 'Effectively, they are producers as well as hosts. They
can read what's happening in the moment. They can constantly
see the show in their heads. And they're just very funny, very
smart and very easy to work with.'

I'm actually blushing a bit now.

Me too.

One of the other key parts of the second incarnation of Takeaway is The End of the Show Show, which is always an enormous amount of work work. Right from the first one, the plan was that each show would finish with a performance that us two got heavily – and, with any luck, comedically – involved in. It could be anything from breakdancing to brass bands, or magic to musicals, and for the first show of the relaunch, we decided we needed someone who could sing, dance and be funny.

There was only one man for the job – Robert Peter Williams. Or Robbie Williams, to you and me.

When we asked Robbie, he reminded us about two musical Christmas sketches we'd done with him a few years earlier. His response was that they'd gone so well, he didn't want to do anything that wasn't up to that standard.

ROBBIE: 'The way we did those Christmas sketches completely changed the way I view what I do. They changed my professional life. Being in the same circle and in the same work sphere as the boys, seeing their work ethic and their love for the medium was a revelation.

Those sketches also reaffirmed for me who I actually was and why I first fell in love with entertainment.

I felt like, "Oh, this is me! I'm not 2am, I'm half-past eight!" It reminded me of the kind of sketches that we loved when we were growing up and it really really touched me deeply.'

Wow. That's lovely. And also, we're nicking 'We're not 2am, we're half-past eight' as our new catchphrase.

– Filming 'Who Shot Simon Cowell?' with some bloke called David Walliams. –

– Drying off after our *Singin' in the Rain* performance. (Also 'Mr and Mr August' for our ill-fated 'Ant and Dec's Sexy Calendar' project.) –

– The first ever End Of The Show Show with Robbie Williams Willian

Anyway, we were determined that the first End of the Show Show of the new series should be huge.

We found out that the Singin' in the Rain musical was coming back to the West End and that, as part of the show, they made it rain on stage, so we thought if we could replicate that then the forecast looked bright, with outbreaks of something special with Robbie Williams.

We went to pitch him the idea in person. We told him about the raining on stage and how we thought it was a chance for the three of us to create something really unique and, crucially, we also took biscuits, which are the secret to any successful pitch in the TV industry.

In the end, he said two things: 'If you two like it, I trust you. Let's do it.'

Followed by: 'Does anyone mind if I have the last chocolate Hobnob?'

ROBBIE: 'Secretly, I was worried about the choreography. After Take That, I'd made a promise to myself that I'd never do that again. But I knew I had to get it right for the lads.'

So, after weeks of rehearsals, we were ready. But the thing about The End of the Show Show is that Takeaway is 90 minutes of live TV where we have to remember a million things and then, when you get to the last part of the show, you have to do the toughest thing of all – a huge (and hopefully show-stopping) performance where there's no margin for error.

It wasn't the easiest set to perform on either – there were gallons of water everywhere, along with dancers, and umbrellas being swung left, right and centre. Robbie kicked it off brilliantly, then us two came in, dressed in yellow

sou'westers, and stole his thunder.

Nice weather pun.

Thank you kindly.

And it was all topped off by us two throwing buckets of water in Robbie's face. He was such a great sport and just the perfect person to do that routine with.

> ROBBIE: 'It's just an honour to be involved, I genuinely mean that. Whether I'm the butt of the joke or making the joke, I don't care. It's the end result that's the most important thing. It's about trying to create moments of magic that last forever.
>
> With other people and other TV shows, obviously I want it to be the best for me, but with Ant and Dec, I have a responsibility to my friendship and their professionalism to pull off what they're asking me to do.
>
> I love those two and I just want it to be the best it can be, for them.'

He did the singing, all we really did was dance about a bit then throw a bucket of water in his face.

Robbie's performance also set the bar pretty high high for future End of the Show Shows.

Over the last few years, we've been really fortunate with some of the performances we've done. From gymnastics with *BGT* winners Spelbound, to Riverdance, to Jess Glynne, to Take That, it's one of the things we're most proud of since we brought the show back.

Having Ed Sheeran on was really exciting for us. We were performing with him and the Royal Marines band, and we'd spent weeks learning how to play the trumpet and trombone parts. The whole idea was that we'd play with the Marines and then Ed would walk out and 'spoil' our performance – partly because we had 'boot polish' (black lipstick) on our lips that 'someone' (Ed) had sneaked onto our instruments before we came out.

So far, so good. But when it came to our big moment on the night, playing a trumpet and trombone live on national television, there was a big problem – the black lipstick made our lips so dry that we sounded terrible. The first few bars did not go according to plan, we could barely get a note out of those instruments. Eventually, our dry lips got a bit of moisture back and frankly, after that, there was no excuse for the fact that we sounded terrible, but we did at least make Ed laugh and put him off his performance.

Another End of the Show Show was in 2013 with Michael Bublé. In the week leading up to him appearing, we just couldn't figure out what the finale should be. Obviously, we knew that, like Robbie, he's a brilliant showman and someone who can do jokes and have a laugh, but we were stumped about how to make the most of that. We were sat in a room with our producers and writers and everyone was firing ideas out, but nothing quite clicked, and then some genius said, 'Why don't we go to the pub?'

I didn't mean, why don't we go to the pub right now?

I meant, why don't we go to the pub in The End of the Show Show?

And the idea took off from there – we would sneak off to the pub during ol' Mickey Bubbles' performance, then he would work out that we'd gone and make his way through the backstage area, out of the studio and across the road to the pub to join us, all while he was singing his track. We pitched it to Michael and he loved the whole thing – except the bit where we called him Mickey Bubbles, that went down less well.

But then we started thinking about his performance and the big question was: How are we going to get to the pub as quickly as possible?

Fortunately, our star guest announcer on that week's show was some bloke called Lewis Hamilton, who has done the odd bit of driving down the years. Our other guest that night was Simon Cowell, so we got a golf buggy and, while Mickey Bubbles sang his little heart out, Lewis would drive us two and Simon to the pub.

It came to the dress rehearsal and everyone had arrived in the studio to give it a go. All of the elements were in place for a live performance that travelled out of the studio and across the road to a pub. We had even made special arrangements to stop traffic outside the studio to make sure we could all cross the road in a golf buggy.

I mean, 'we' didn't make those arrangements, obviously, we wouldn't know where to start – there's probably a lot of forms involved. Some grown-ups in high-vis jackets did it for us.

As planned, during Michael's performance we jumped in the buggy and we were off. But there was a problem. A big problem. Our journey was supposed to last for most of Michael's three-minute performance, but then we realised something.

We had a Formula One world champion doing the driving, so we got there in about 12 seconds. Even the cameras couldn't keep up, so we had to say something no one's ever said to Lewis Hamilton before: 'Can you drive slower, please?'

Lewis got the message and, by the time we actually did it on the live show, me, Ant, Simon Cowell and Lewis Hamilton enjoyed a lovely jaunty drive to the pub in a golf buggy, while

Michael Bublé (eventually) followed and we all ended up in the pub, ready to do karaoke together.

It was one of the nights where you just thought, 'I can't believe this is my job.'

> SIMON: 'I always have a good time on their show. I don't think of it as work when I get a call to do something with those two, especially when it's something crazy. Drive across the set with Lewis Hamilton? You're not going to say no to that, are you?
>
> They even did a sketch called "Who Shot Simon Cowell?" – when they asked me about it, I said yes immediately. I don't normally love doing that kind of thing, but I know if they're involved, it will be smart and funny, and I'll have a good time doing it. And that's down to the fact that we not only share a friendship, but also a lot of respect.'

Did you hear that? Respect! I knew someone would respect us one day. It only took 30 years. . .

Arguably the most memorable End of the Show Show we ever did did was towards the end of the series.

Do you think the joke's wearing a bit thin thin now?

Not a chance chance.
     At the time, there was a show on ITV2 called *The Big Reunion*, which was being made by our old mate from *cd:uk*, Phil Mount (the one who told Bono he'd had a 'Beautiful Day'). *The Big Reunion* was all about getting the biggest pop acts from the 1990s and early 2000s and bringing them back together.

*Which was why they used the words 'big' and 'reunion' in the title.
     It featured all the acts we'd had on cd:uk 15 years earlier –*

*B*Witched, Liberty X, Atomic Kitten, Blue and Five – and it was a big ratings hit.*

We decided to have Atomic Kitten, Blue and Five on to do The End of the Show Show and initially we weren't going to get too involved, but then a few people started tweeting us, saying, 'When are PJ & Duncan going to be on The Big Reunion?' As a laugh, I said to Dec, 'Shall we do it?' and he said . . .

'Yeah, we should.'

And I said, 'We could, couldn't we?'

And he said, 'Can we still remember the routine?'

And I said, 'I don't know, but let's definitely recount this exchange word for word in a book in seven years' time.'

Then he said, 'OK then, but let's stop now.'

The next day we went into the Takeaway office and told them we were 'Ready To Rhumble'. The team sprang into action. Our stylist Toni Porter set about sourcing our original outfits – oversized hockey shirts, caps, the works. Gemma Nightingale, our producer, found us a backing track to perform to and we taught the original dance routine to our backing dancers, who were ready to help us wreck the mic . . . Psyche!

When it came to the show itself, Five, Atomic Kitten and Blue performed first and went down a storm. We were waiting backstage, watching on a monitor, and we could see the studio audience were revelling in the nostalgia. We'd kept the fact we'd be performing a secret from the audience and even actively played down the idea during the show, so it would make for a big surprise when we appeared.

We were dressed in our original 'Rhumble' outfits, gripping

our mics tightly, desperately trying not to wreck them too early. With palms sweating and hearts racing, we climbed the stairs to wait for our cue. Blue finished their set with their arms aloft, singing 'One love is all we need', and the audience cheered and clapped. Then a familiar voice boomed out: 'Let's Get Ready To Rhumbllllllllllle' and we launched ourselves onto the stage. The noise from the audience went up a level and we windmilled and rhumbled as if our lives depended on it. The response in the studio made the hairs on the back of our necks stand on end.

It caught us completely by surprise – we couldn't believe it.

In the green room after the show, we were having a few drinks with The Big Reunion *bands talking about their show and reminiscing about the old days when they were regular guests on sm:tv. Antony Costa from Blue came over, clutching his phone, and said, 'Have you seen this?' I wondered what he was going to show me; I can get a bit squeamish and hoped it was nothing gross. You never know with Costa. He turned his screen towards me and showed me: 'Let's Get Ready To Rhumble' was climbing the iTunes chart by the minute. PJ & Duncan were experiencing a strange sensation – people were paying to listen to their music.*

For the next few days, the song kept climbing and then, before we knew what was happening, we were both round at mine, listening to the Top 40 chart show on Radio 1 on a Sunday night – it was just like the old days.

Except we weren't sat in the back of a Toyota Previa, munching on a Ginsters pasty and hearing the words, 'Unfortunately, PJ & Duncan entered at number 72 so won't be part of this countdown.'

We were genuinely nervous listening to that countdown, not because we had anything riding on it, but because we were so touched by the public's response and we both hoped the story could have the perfect ending.

They got to the top ten and we still hadn't heard where 'Rhumble' was. They went past number nine, where it had peaked in 1994 (as our highest-ever single), and then we were into the top five, still no mention, the top three, still no mention, and then we heard those magic words, those words we thought we'd never, ever hear . . .

'And this week's number one is PJ & Duncan, with "Let's Get Ready To Rhumble".'

Unbelievable. As the photo proves, the look on our faces is best described as 'jubilant disbelief'. It was incredible. PJ & Duncan, an act who had so often been described as a load of number two, actually had a number one, 19 years after the song was released. We decided to give any royalties we'd receive to Childline, so in all of this madness, some good actually came out of it.

I also think our relationship with that song, and our pop career in general, changed there and then. For a long time, it was something we wanted to leave behind, something we were embarrassed about, but now it felt like enough time had passed, and we'd had enough success as presenters, that we could finally, properly, have a laugh and embrace our pop star selves.

And that was just 19 short years after everyone else was laughing at our pop star selves.

Talk about fashionably late . . .

One of the other crucial aspects of Takeaway 2.0 was doing the last show of the series from an amazing holiday destination. We broadcast it from a cruise ship in Barcelona in 2016, Walt Disney World Resort, Florida, in 2017 and Universal Studios Florida in 2018. Building up to a massive finale gives us a 'story' to tell throughout the series, a story that gets more and more exciting

- Hands up if you can't quite believe LGRTR eventually got to number 1. -

- Harry Potter And The Half Pint Geordies. -

Rehearsing for our 2017 finale in Disney World at crack of dawn before the park opened. -

– With star of stage, screen a
stupid hats, Stephen Mulhern

– Stephen: 'Why did no one tell me it was "Come To Work As Pac-Man Day"' –

every week and, most importantly, it allows us to give people the holiday of a lifetime.

And those finales, especially the ones we did in Florida, were just something else. It's a crazy week. We take the whole team out there, which is around 120 people, and we often rehearse from 5am, before all the parks open – there's just nothing like it, especially sharing it with hundreds of lovely people.

And Ant.

There are so many other things we love about Takeaway that we could fill another book with them: the tour we did in 2014, all the audience surprises, the Happiest Minute of the Week, Singalong Live, the weekly comedy dramas we do, I could go on.

And, of course, there's Ant versus Dec, hosted by self-proclaimed star of stage and screen, Stephen Mulhern.

STEPHEN MULHERN: 'When I first started doing Ant versus Dec, it was amazing, another level to anything I'd done before. The boys have been incredibly generous to me, both in terms of their time and the material. They think nothing of saying, Stephen should do that gag, it'll be funnier. And that's the most enormous compliment.'

I just like having 'enormous' in any sentence that describes me.

Stephen makes us laugh so much though – our relationship with him started when he hosted *Britain's Got More Talent* and it's grown into something we really cherish, and that's become a key part of the show.

We have such a huge affection for him. He's the first person since Cat that we've shared so much screen time with and we wouldn't have it any other way. It takes a lot for me and Dec to let someone in like that, but we get the biggest kick out of having Stephen on the show.

> STEPHEN: 'I always watch them rehearse on Saturday Night Takeaway. I could just sit in my dressing room, but I come in early to sit in the studio and watch them work. They make TV look so easy, but people don't realise how hard they work to make it look that easy.'

Did you know he watched us rehearse?

No. I always wondered who that bloke with the dark glasses and fake beard holding a magic set was . . .

We genuinely love Stephen, though. Not only is he a lovely man, but the three of us share a lot of the same influences and sensibilities, and Stephen is also a great live presenter. We have complete trust in him, which means we can relax and muck about with him on air – that's so much fun. He's hilarious. We love having him around.

Having said all of that, one of my favourite Ant versus Dec memories doesn't actually involve Stephen.

I like it already.

We were doing an Ant versus Dec back in 2017 called 'The Floor Is Lava', where we both dressed up as dinosaurs, and the brilliant Chris Kamara was commentating. What happens on most TV shows, especially when you're a guest rather than a regular, is that you camera-check your clothes – which means you show them to the director to make sure they don't strobe on camera, or clash with the set or anything. Like the true pro he is, when he arrived that day, Chris very kindly said to the producer, 'I've brought three suits with me, so you can camera-check them all.'

The producer took a deep breath and said, 'Thanks, Chris, but I'm afraid none of those is quite right.'

Chris, ever the cheerful soul, politely asked why not.

The producer looked at him with a completely straight face and said, 'Because you're going to be wearing caveman furs.'

Amazing.

Of course, we've just finished a series of Saturday Night Takeaway as we write this book and it was arguably our most eventful one ever. We did some unforgettable things, like giving away a house—

Still can't believe we pulled that off.

—our first-ever double Undercover, when we got Bradley Walsh 15 years after the first time we caught him out. We also did a brand-new type of hidden-camera stunt where we dressed up as pandas in London Zoo.

Obviously, as Newcastle fans, it had to be a black and white animal.

We wanted to do something on the show that had kids at the centre of it. Children make up a huge part of *Takeaway*'s viewers and, in the end, we went for the obvious choice – dress up as pandas that could 'talk'. And we got some great stuff on the day – the kids who engaged with the pandas were amazing.

You wouldn't know this from watching the show, but we also had our fair share of kids who got completely freaked out and a couple even ran off. Ideally in that situation, we'd whip off the panda heads we were wearing and say, 'Don't be scared, it's only Ant and Dec!' But it took an hour to get the make-up and costume on and off, so that wasn't an option.

I have to say, I can fully sympathise with those kids who got freaked out – if I was eight years old and I went to the zoo, only for the pandas to start talking to me, I would be freaked out of my tiny little mind too.

To be honest, even if we could have taken off the panda heads and revealed it was us, that would have only freaked them out even more.

But the thing we'll always remember about series 16 of Saturday Night Takeaway is, of course, when the whole country was brought to a standstill due to the coronavirus pandemic.

The minute it started looking serious, we knew we wanted to try to put a smile on people's faces during a very difficult time. To do that, we'd stay on the air as long as government guidelines allowed us to.

We always do seven shows a series and, by the time we got to show four, things were changing very quickly. The moment the Prime Minister banned large gatherings, we realised our only option with show five was to do it without a studio audience and with a small but dedicated crew.

Even then, we weren't sure if it was the right thing to do. We sat around with our team and talked it through – in the end, we decided that, as long as we were observing those vital guidelines, making the TV show for people to watch gave us the chance to offer them some small respite from what was going on.

Once we'd made the decision, we went to work putting together the best bloody show we could. We had our Undercover on Bradley Walsh to show, we did an Ant versus Dec where we ran around an empty studio, and we got Olly Murs for The End of the Show Show.

That was especially important, and Olly was just perfect. All week, we asked people to send in footage of themselves singing and dancing to his track 'Dance With Me Tonight'. We wanted to include as many people as we could and produce the biggest End of the Show Show in the most trying of circumstances for everyone. We thought that, just because people had to stay at home and self-isolate, it didn't mean we couldn't smile, sing and dance. It didn't mean we had to stay in and be scared; we could come together and keep in touch with one another to try to get through the most terrifying of times.

We didn't know it at the time, but this would be our last show before the country went into lockdown. The day before it went live, we sat down with the producers, who had compiled a tape of the videos people had sent in. We had been inundated with footage, there were tens of thousands of submissions, but obviously we couldn't use every single one, so we had to decide on an order of preference. It was the first time we'd watched the footage that had been sent in. It included videos from children, carers, nurses, police officers, the fire service, elderly people in care homes – every walk of life imaginable. About ten of us sat and watched the compilation until the very end and, when we looked up, we were all in tears.

It was a privilege to be on air that week and we felt like the show had a real purpose, to try to unite people and reflect what was going on and how people were feeling all over the country. But, most importantly, to show people that they weren't alone; we were all feeling fear and uncertainty, but it was OK to feel that way, because we were all in it together.

The show itself was one of the weirdest we've ever done, because our studio audience are such a huge part of Takeaway.

But by the time we got to Olly's performance, it felt like one of the proudest and most moving moments in our 30-year career.

When we came off, we went to our dressing rooms, got showered, changed and sanitised, had another little cry together, and then said goodbye. And, as we write this part of the book now, eight weeks later, we haven't seen each other since.

And the feedback we had, the messages we got afterwards, were unlike anything we've ever known. And that meant a great deal to both of us.

After the show with no audience, the plan had been to put out two 'Best of's for the last two episodes and we'd even recorded links for them the week before.

But then on the Monday after show five, the whole country went into lockdown and we wanted to do something to reflect that – something to show that, just like everyone else, we were at home too.

So we did the last two shows from our homes, hosting them via our mobile phones. It wasn't quite the finale we'd imagined, but we wanted something for the people who make Saturday Night Takeaway what it is, the people we began this chapter talking about and the people who mean the most to us: our incredible audience.

And after years of them welcoming us into their homes on a Saturday night, it was nice to be able to return the favour.

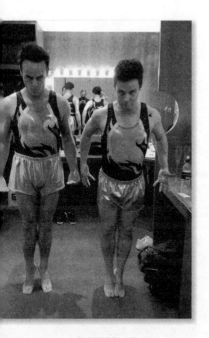

– Spelbound EOTSS: 'Well we're never going to need these gold shorts again, are we?' –

– *Takeaway* producer Pete working on a couple of dodgy pilots. –

– NYC. 'Look, it's those two blokes off the telly!' –

Ed Sheeran: 'That's where you're wrong.' –

7

I'M A CELEBRITY... GET ME OUT OF HERE!

I'M A CELEBRITY . . . GET ME OUT OF HERE! ANT AND DEC
CALL SHEET:

02.30	ALARM CALL
03.00	LEAVE HOTEL AND DRIVE TO SITE
03.30	ARRIVE ON SITE
03.45	RECORD VOICEOVERS
04.00	SCRIPT MEETING
04.30	WATCH SHOW
05.30	SCRIPT REWRITES
06.00	WARDROBE AND MAKE-UP
06.30	TRAVEL TO STUDIO AND REHEARSE
07.00	LIVE SHOW
08.30	LIVE SHOW FINISHES, RETURN TO OFFICE
09.00	BREAKFAST
09.30	SCRIPT MEETING FOR BUSHTUCKER TRIAL
10.00	SHOOT BUSHTUCKER TRIAL
12.00	WRAP BUSHTUCKER TRIAL
12.15	LEAVE SITE
12.45	ARRIVE BACK AT HOTEL
	LEISURE TIME
18.30	GO TO BED

That's what's <u>supposed</u> to happen, but I don't think we've stuck to that schedule once in almost 20 years. It usually goes awry when Dec gets in the car at 03.15, because he's always late. For everything.

That's not true. I'm not late for <u>everything</u>. I always get to the bridge on time for the big '*I'm a Celebrity* . . . Get Me Out of Heeeeeere!' at 7am.

I'll give you that, but you're late for every other part of that schedule and you've basically been keeping me waiting for 30 years.

Happy anniversary!

Shut up! You were even late for writing this chapter.

OK, OK, let's just tell the lovely reader about *I'm a Celebrity . . . Get Me Out of Here!*, shall we?
I can still remember the moment we were first pitched the show. It was at a meeting with the show's original executive producers, Natalka Znak and Richard Cowles. Richard is still in charge of it today and, in our opinion, is the true king of the jungle.

Hopefully he's reading this, and we can get a bit of a lie-in next series.
We both thought the same thing when we heard the pitch: firstly, that it was a great idea that we'd be mad to turn down; and, secondly, that the incredibly long and very weird title would be changed before it went on air.
We were half right.

The campmates for the first series back in 2002 were Tony Blackburn, Tara Palmer-Tomkinson, Christine Hamilton, Nell McAndrew, Rhona Cameron, Darren Day, Nigel Benn and Uri Geller, and it's easy to forget now, what with it being nearly two decades ago, but the show got off to quite a slow start. The ratings weren't great, and we weren't quite sure how we fitted into the whole thing. We played our links quite straight, mainly because it was all new and no one quite knew what was going on. We weren't sure it was our place to be funny about celebrities in a jungle.

Thank God we didn't stick with that strategy.
But in the second week, things really picked up. Darren and Tara had a fiery and flirtatious relationship punctuated by some fascinating conversations (also known as blazing rows), Rhona had a big rant about the whole camp, and suddenly the tabloids started covering it and GMTV began talking about it (although they failed to use the term 'Fun in

the Sun', which I thought was a mistake . . .).

Let's not bring up our biggest fight again, shall we?

At the end of it, the even-tempered and relentlessly lovely Tony Blackburn was a worthy winner.

Side note: We wore suits for the final. Full-on black suits. We went down into the jungle wearing actual suits.

What were we thinking?

On the plus side, the show was a massive hit and has never really looked back. The difference between that first series and the show now is like chalk and . . . a kangaroo's anus. Series 1 was filmed in northern Queensland, close to a town called Tully, near Cairns, which is much further north and more tropical than where we shoot now. And, frankly, just like the first series of *Pop Idol*, we were making it up as we went along.

When I tell you one of the Bushtucker Trials involved former middleweight boxing champion Nigel Benn sitting under a tree in the dark for an hour, you get the idea of how basic it was.

One thing we did come up with was shouting, '*I'm a Celebrity* . . . Get Me Out of Heeeeerreeeeee!' on the bridge at the start of the show and, apart from us two, that's pretty much the only thing that's survived since the first series.

For series 2, ITV found a new site, near a small town called Murwillumbah, further south on the Queensland–New South Wales border. They had acres of land and they essentially built a small village from scratch. It houses the editing suites, production offices, catering, medical facilities, the transport department and, most importantly of all, a camp for famous people to live in for three weeks.

With such a massive site, the possibilities became endless, so the show just grew bigger and bigger.

Series 2 came eight months after the first one and was won by Phil 'Tuffers' Tufnell, but it was series 3 when we really found our feet in terms of doing comedy links every night.

And it was no wonder, because that third series just about had it all – a love story between Katie Price and Peter Andre, who famously went on to get married; eventual winner Kerry Katona (who enjoyed the archetypal jungle journey, going from terrified of everything to game for anything); Neil 'Razor' Ruddock (who claimed he'd 'never been hungry before'); and one of the finest contestants in the show's history, John Lydon, aka Johnny Rotten, aka the lead singer of the bloody Sex bloody Pistols.

At first, we simply couldn't believe he'd agreed to do the show. To be honest, even now, all these years later, I can't quite believe he did it.

For the first few days, I'm not sure he could either.

But John was fascinating; he turned out to be a huge animal lover and immersed himself in the tropical rainforest environment. And he was great value, even if we did have the occasional tricky moment with him.

Who'd have thought we'd have tricky moments with the lead singer of the Sex Pistols on live TV?

Me.

Yeah, me too.
Probably the trickiest of all was one morning when we went into camp to announce who'd be the next to leave.

Every morning, we make a hurried and wobbly journey across three rickety rope bridges in the baking sun, with only a cameraman and a floor manager for company.

Please, don't call us heroes.

And then we arrive in camp, ready to face the celebs, and no matter what's been going on for the last 24 hours, every time you go in there, there's something in the air.

And that something is BO.
　　They absolutely stink, the lot of them. It's not their fault; they've been bathing in dirty water and sitting round a campfire for weeks on end, but every year they really do smell very, very bad.

And the 2019 series was even worse than normal. Because of the Australian bushfires, the campmates had a gas burner, rather than an open fire. Normally, the campfire can conceal some of the BO, but not that year.

It was like when the smoking ban came in for pubs. Once the smell of smoke disappeared you realised one thing: 'This pub stinks.'

Anyway, we digress. They stink, that's the point – and this was a day when an extra stink was about to be kicked up, thanks to Mr Lydon. We were in camp and doing our usual announcement about who would be leaving that day, 'It's not you, it might be you' – it's a classic routine. Then I got to John, who had made no secret of the fact he'd had enough of the camp, the trials and, more crucially, the other celebrities, and was ready to go. I said the perfectly simple words, 'John, they've decided . . . it's not you.' And, quick as a flash, he replied:
　　*'Oh, f*****g c**t!'*

My jaw hit the floor and I nearly dropped my cue cards in the fire. I mumbled some sort of half telling-off along the lines of, 'Hey, come on now. Come on, John.'

Then, after being silent up to this point, the producers started shouting in my earpiece, 'Apologise! APOLOGISE!'

I thought, 'What have I got to be sorry about?'

Then I realised they meant apologise on John's behalf.

I jumped in and immediately said sorry. A few days later, John took matters into his own hands and walked off the show. He went back to the Versace hotel, where he spent days on end screaming the c-word: 'Complementary room service'.

And, interesting point for all you fact fans, thanks to John we now have a five-second delay on the reveals we do in camp, so we can bleep out any other potty-mouthed punks.

The thing about people swearing on TV is that – and this is a scientific fact – it's very funny. That's why apologising for it can be hard, because you want to laugh, just like we did with Slash on cd:uk four years earlier.

But it's another advantage of being a double act: one of you can apologise for swearing, while the other can concentrate on not laughing at the swearing. It's perfect.

That series was also when we started working with a writer who's still with us 16 years later, Andy Milligan. As well as working on all our TV shows, Andy's helping us write this book and, as a result, he knows more about our last 30 years together than anyone else, except maybe us two, right, Andy?

'I definitely know more than you two.'

– Wearing suits for the first *I'm A Celebrity* final
and looking very cool, thank you very much. –

– Agreeing our
second exclusive ITV
contract with Claudia
Rosencrantz and St
Nigel Pickard, not, as it
would appear, signing a
wedding register. –

– With our writer Andy. He's allowed
to touch us once a year. –

And that's the last we'll be hearing from Andy.

That John Lydon story sums up just what a bizarre and unique job I'm a Celebrity is and it's one we love so, so much.

The next one will be the 20th — yes, I said TWENTIETH — series of the show. It's funny to think, but when you look back at the rest of our career, I'm a Celeb is probably closest to sm:tv, because it's all about quick, funny, live links in between various pieces of footage. And it also has its fair share of double entendres.

And everyone knows how hard they can be.

Oo-er.

You can't help yourself, can you?

As well as all of those similarities, I'm a Celeb also (in case you hadn't noticed) doesn't have a studio audience. It would be very weird if it did, but what that means is that the crew of 20 to 30 (mainly Aussie) people in our little treehouse become the audience. I mean, they're an audience who are being paid to be there, but they're the only one we've got.

They're also a big part of why we're so relaxed about doing the show. Part of that relaxation is that with *Takeaway* or *BGT*, we're used to doing a show in the evening, so we often arrive at the studio 12 hours before we're on air and spend a whole day preparing and rehearsing, but with *I'm a Celebrity*, we're live on the telly less than five hours after we wake up.

Plus, we have an amazing team working on the show, especially if they're reading this. In fact, if they're reading this, they're the best team in the history of television.

We're so relaxed that it seems completely abstract that there could be 10 million people watching when we're just

mucking about in a treehouse. It mainly feels like a small handful of people are paying attention to what we're doing, but at least we're making them laugh.

In that sense, it's more like our pop career.

Social media has made a huge difference to the show, too. *I'm a Celeb* is the perfect programme to 'second screen', which is a technical term I once heard a geek use that means 'Look at your phone while watching telly'. That way, the audience can comment on any part of the show they like – from Dingo Dollar Challenges to letters from home to why we have our watches covered up during the Bushtucker Trials.

(Which – for the millionth time – is so the celebs don't know the time. That comes up on Twitter a lot.)

Social media also means we can reply to viewers during the live show and tell them that we don't want to just take our watches off (which is always their next question after they ask why we cover our watches). Often, there might be something in a VT we've missed (a funny facial expression from a celeb or a throwaway moment in a Bushtucker Trial, for instance) and, if people tweet us about it, we'll refer to it in the following link so that we look like we haven't missed it at all and, actually, for your information, we're very clever thank you very much.

One of our favourite things about I'm a Celeb is that it works so many different muscles in terms of performance. Obviously, it's live, so there's all the discipline that comes with that: doing the voting info, going into camp, making the announcements, doing interviews when people leave. But there's also the small matter of ten minutes of live comedy every episode, all based around what's happened in the last 24 hours.

One of the highlights is when we arrive in the dead of night and take a cup of English breakfast tea (me) and a cup of green tea (Dec) into our script meeting at 4am. Our writers, Andy Milligan and Mark Busk-Cowley, have been working through the night on gags, so we go through it all with them, and the four of us keep rewriting and honing right up until we're on air.

And those jokes we have prepared have got more involved and more complicated as the years have gone on. The props in particular get increasingly ridiculous – and because the majority of what we do is reactive, they all have to be made and sourced in the middle of the night in Australia, which makes things doubly difficult.

We've requested every prop you can imagine – we've had doors made, full-sized dummies of ourselves, T-shirts with our names on, tiny pairs of jeans, a 'jungle iPod' – and that's before you take into account the stuff people have to track down. Like a snooker table, a copy of Nelson Mandela's autobiography or, my personal favourite, a shopping trolley. Finding a shopping trolley at 4am in the middle of the Australian rainforest is not easy – on this occasion, it involved some poor runner driving 40 minutes to the nearest supermarket, patiently waiting for it to open and then sweet-talking the manager into lending us one of their trolleys.

I thought they just nicked it out of the car park?

No, definitely not.

But the links we do are so, so important to us and, hopefully, to the show. First and foremost, it's our job to tell the story of the last 24 hours in camp, but also to try to be as funny as we can, as often as we can.

– A small business we run on the side when we're in Australia. –

– A couple of slippery jungle creatures . . . holding two lizards. –

– Worried there wouldn't be a topless picture of us drinking tea in a swimming pool? You can now relax. –

– Watching Newcastle United play while Ant pretends they've actually scored a goal. –

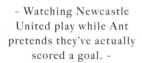

One of the things people say when they stop us in the street is:

'I can't wait for *I'm a Celebrity*! I only watch it for your links, I fast-forward all the jungle bits!'

And I always think, 'Thank you, but that doesn't make any sense, all our links relate to what's happening in the camp.'

It's the equivalent of saying, 'I love watching Match of the Day, but I only watch Gary Lineker's bits, I fast-forward all the football.'

Another thing people often say is:

'How would you two do in the jungle, as campmates?'

Well, we've thought about it and I actually think Ant would do really well. Definitely top three.

Top three? I'd win it!

You might be right. You're very outdoorsy, you get on with people, you're quite patient, you'd give the trials a good go, you'd eat anything. I think you'd do really, really well.

That's very kind, thank you, Declan.

What about me, how do you think I'd do in the jungle?

Well, let's just say I think you'd be brilliant on Strictly.

What?

I'm just not sure you're cut out for I'm a Celeb.

Why not?

*Where shall I start? Because you're the kind of person
who would say, 'No thank you' and walk after three days,
because you've got a short fuse, because you're not that into
the outdoors, you get grumpy when you're hungry . . .*

I suppose when you put it like that . . .

It's certainly not an easy show to do and it's an incredible
operation behind the scenes too. The celebs are monitored
within an inch of their lives from the moment they land in
Australia. You'll be amazed at how meticulously planned
it is before they even get into the jungle. Although we
shouldn't really reveal any of that, should we?

Sod it, it's our book!

Good point.

They fly in with a chaperone and then, alongside a
security guard, different celebs are taken to different hotels
on Australia's Gold Coast. On the journey there, they get
to make one phone call – on speaker phone so the
chaperone can hear it – and then, after that, their phone
is taken away from them and locked in the vault when they
arrive at the hotel.

*'You have the right to remain silent, but anything you do say
may stop you being allowed into the jungle.'*

Then the security guard does a full sweep of the celeb's
room, making sure the landline only takes incoming calls
and that there is no WiFi available. Then they go through
the celeb's luggage and confiscate any devices.

It's like something out of a Bond film – albeit a Bond film where someone eats a lot of buffet food and isn't allowed to go on Instagram or ring their mum.

A few of them always manage to give the chaperone the slip. Boris Johnson's dad Stanley ran away to go to the beach, Caitlyn Jenner legged it to the shops and Amir Khan managed to befriend a boy who worked in a bakery across the road from the Versace hotel and persuaded him to let Amir use his phone.

It's that level of determination that makes you a boxing champion.

And probably gets you free iced buns.

Clothes-wise, they're only allowed to bring three sets of swimwear and three sets of underwear, but what happens every year – especially with young blokes who go on the show – is that they bring boxer shorts that are covered in logos and branding. And then, for advertising reasons, they're not allowed to wear them, so then someone has to go to the local supermarket and buy them three pairs of cheap, unbranded pants, which is what they wear in camp.

Nothing says showbiz like the words 'supermarket pants'.

And then once they and their supermarket shreddies actually get into camp, well, that's when the fun really starts. And the great leveller every year, no matter who's in there, no matter how famous they are, is our old friends the Bushtucker Trials.

If you don't know what a Bushtucker Trial is then I'll eat one of the campmate's hats: they've become an iconic part of British telly and in a nutshell—

That won't be the last mention of nuts . . .

—they are a daily challenge where celebs get the chance to win meals for themselves and their fellow campmates. And those challenges can involve anything from live crocodiles to turkey testicles.

Told you.

The trials are normally pre-recorded and, when we first started doing them live, it almost gave us a heart attack. The pre-recorded ones that get edited down were incredibly time-consuming, thanks to indecisive celebs, health and safety briefings and the sheer scale of them, so we thought doing one live would be a nightmare.

And for the first few years, we were right. Celebs would say no to them, so it was always a very edge-of-the-seat half-hour of TV for us to host, where things can – and often did – go wrong.

Of course, the audience loves it when things go wrong – and we love a bit of unpredictability more than most presenters – but this was quite nerve-racking. There's a world of difference between unpredictable and just downright bad television. The live trials began in series 3, and when former All Saint Natalie Appleton was voted to do it in series 4, our worst fears were realised – she couldn't make up her mind. She was in, then she was out, then she was in – it was like a jungle remix of the hokey cokey.

We've had some truly crazy trials down the years. Favourites, Declan?

Easy. Gillian McKeith. 2010. Live trial. To refresh your memory, Gillian had been chosen for trial after trial after

With our security guard and driver, Junior. (He's the one in the middle.) –

– 'If we put wood round the edge of this plasma TV, we can call it a "jungle telly." –

– After our Celebrity Cyclone trial for charity in 2011. –

trial that series – and done terribly in almost all of them – so it was inevitable viewers would decide she would do the live one.

Before every live trial, in our script meeting, we go through the contingency plans for what happens if the celeb refuses to take part. Obviously, it's happening live, unlike all the other trials, so we need a plan B if we have to fill half an hour of live telly. That year, we paid special attention to the contingency plan, because we knew Gillian wouldn't do it.

As someone said at the time: 'She definitely won't go through that s**t.'

Which, ironically, was the exact opposite of what she normally did for a living . . .

But going into the live show, we knew exactly what we would do if she refused – we had classic live trials lined up to play out and talking points to go through with the other celebs – and we were 100 per cent positive she would refuse. Then, unexpected thing number one happened.

She didn't refuse.

We called out her name and she made her way towards me and Dec.

And then unexpected thing number two happened.

She fainted.

Live on national television.

While Medic Bob rushed in with oxygen, we looked at our cue cards and, strangely enough, we didn't have one that said, 'What to do if Gillian faints live on national television.' *I ended up saying, 'Er, I think it's best if we go to a break right now and give Gillian the attention she needs. We'll find out if she can do it after the break. See you in a few minutes.'*

In the end, Linford 'The Lunchbox' Christie did the trial, but in a lot of the coverage in the papers and on social media people wondered, 'Was she putting it on? Was the whole thing an act?'

We couldn't possibly comment.

A lot of people <u>could</u> comment that she was putting it on, but we are NOT two of those people.

Definitely not.

I still don't know how we kept a straight face though.

Looking back at the footage, I'm not sure we did.
   But the most important thing was—

That Gillian was OK?

No, that it gave us plenty of material for the links.
   Gillian certainly brought a lot to that series – not least a specially made pair of knickers that had secret compartments which helped her to smuggle in contraband spices for the food.

If you could smuggle in something in contraband pants, what would it be?

Ooh, good question. Probably a very small mobile phone. What about you, what little thing would you sneak into camp?

You.

Idiot.

Gillian's trial wasn't the only dicey moment we've had with Bushtucker Trials, though. The following year, and there's no easy way of saying this, a cockroach crawled inside two-time Olympian Fatima Whitbread's head.

It's not a sentence you ever expect to type, but there you go.

It had threatened to happen to someone for years and now it finally had – this cockroach went straight up Fatima's nose and refused to come out. I don't mind telling you, I found it very difficult to watch.

How do you think she felt?

She was remarkable, to be fair, she's a tough lady – and what you don't realise watching the edited version on TV is how long it took to get the little so-and-so out of there. It was up there for quite a while, scratching around. Medic Bob arrived on the scene and shot jets of water up her nostrils with a huge syringe. After lots of sniffing and blowing from Fatima, this live cockroach came flying out of her nose.

I can't lie, I thought I was going to vomit on the spot.

What a trouper you were for getting through it.

As we've said, on I'm a Celeb our job is to be the voice of the audience, to react how we think they would react, but there are certain times – and this was one of them – where you forget you're on TV and just think . . . how can I put this?

'Bloody hell, a live cockroach has just shot out of Fatima Whitbread's nostril!'

Yeah, that's it.

Course, it's not just the celebs who have to endure trials when they're in Australia; we have our fair share of challenges to deal with.

So true. One year, the hotel pool was being cleaned for a whole week.

I was talking about my spider bite. It happened down at the trial clearing, appropriately enough. I woke up the next morning, at 2am, as normal—

Then kept me waiting, as normal.

—and the spider bite had blown up. It looked like I had huge red warts on my finger (as the pictures testify) and I was told I needed to get it looked at when I arrived on site. When I got there, I had to undergo a succession of delicate and complex medical procedures.

Didn't they pop it with a needle?

Yes.
   The medic held the needle steady, then looked at me and said, 'You might feel a bit of a prick.'

Writes itself, doesn't it?
   I thought I'd leave him to it, so I went to ring my mam.
   When I came back 15 minutes later, the door to Dec's and my office was shut. Someone said, 'Dec's taken a turn for the worse' and, when the door opened, I saw three medics standing in a circle, looking down at the floor. One of them was holding an oxygen tank with the mask clamped around Dec's mouth and nose, while another held his legs in the air.

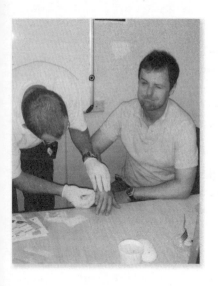

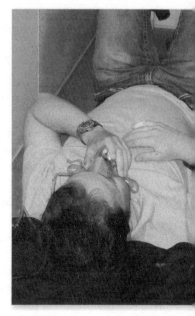

– 'This is my worst O2 experien[ce]
since The BRITs.' –

– 'Smile and say
"showbiz!"' 'No.
It's 3am.' –

– The Bushtucker Trial team all turned up
in the same outfit. Embarrassing. –

I'm not very good with the sight of blood and I nearly passed out, or 'Did a Gillian' as we call it in Oz.

The medics assured me that Dec would be fine, and the oxygen was just to bring him round. I was so relieved that I took several photos with my phone of him lying on the floor.

That was a horrible bite, though. As they were leaving the office, I heard one of the medics say, 'That was one nasty little b*****d.'

They weren't talking about the spider.

What?

While we're on the subject of drama queens, I think one of my favourite-ever contestants came in 2015 with Lady C. How amazing was Lady C?!

She did not give a flying . . . Well, she was a loose cannon, let's put it that way. For those who need reminding, Lady C was Lady Colin Campbell, a socialite and writer whose title came from a short-lived marriage to the 11th Duke of Argyll.

That lady was manna from heaven, the best worst campmate we've ever had. Night after night after night, she just tore strips off everyone: her fellow campmates, the producers, us two – she was a proper firebrand.

She could be lovely too, but she would always have a go at us about the Bushtucker Trials, as if we'd designed them ourselves and then personally cast tens of thousands of votes to make sure she did them. She would always say things like, 'You two are sick, you're twisted individuals.'

She did also offer me and Ant a threesome with her.

Oh God, I forgot about that. Let's just move on, for the sake of everyone in that sentence.

And that was pretty tame, compared to how she spoke to her fellow campmates, although, to be fair, she always said it to their faces. According to her ladyship, Duncan Bannatyne was 'a vain old goat', Brian Friedman was 'a self-important little runt, desperate for attention', and Tony Hadley was 'a dumbo, a chippy oik, a liar and the mouth of diarrhoea'.

Don't forget she also called him 'a fat slob'.

In fact, the only two people she didn't clash with were ex-Newcastle footballer Kieron Dyer and boxing legend Chris Eubank.

I absolutely loved having Chris in there, he's a total one-off, just so watchable. Kieron was struggling one day, and Chris said to him, 'Will you take counsel?' Not, 'Are you OK?' or, 'Do you want to chat?'
It was so lovely and SO Chris Eubank. Imagine it in his voice, 'Will you take counsel?' It was such an endearing moment. He's the perfect I'm a Celeb contestant, because he's utterly unique and he's also a household name. I'd love to be mates with Chris Eubank.

He still calls me every now and then.

What?

He took my number after the show and every now and then he rings up and asks how I am. I remember a while back, you were in America on holiday and an American number popped up on my phone and, thinking it was you, I answered it. It was Chris.

What did he want?

Just checking to see if I wanted to take counsel.

Chris was one of those names that before they even went in, you were just so excited to see what they brought to the show. Probably the best example of that recently was—

Hang on, before we tell them, why don't we give our lovely reader a taste of how we find out who's going to be on the show?

Great idea.

Every year, a month or so before the show starts, we have a meeting to hear the final cast list with the executive producers, Richard Cowles, Tom Gould, Ollie Nash and Micky Van Praagh. Before that meeting, we've had a bit of back and forth in our *I'm a Celeb* WhatsApp group about who's in and who's out, with everyone making suggestions, but this is the big one, the final, definitive list. We get very excited.

And, like any good meeting in telly, there are biscuits.

Micky, Richard, Ollie and Tom sit on one side of a table and we sit on the other. They have laminated, passport photo-sized headshots of the cast face down on the table and, one by one, they turn them over to reveal them. They say to us, 'OK, first one – are you ready?'

We say, 'Yfdves pfftss.'

Which is, 'Yes please!' but through a mouthful of biscuits.

They alternate between the men and the women and then they'll do the late arrivals. And I don't mind telling you, that is one of my favourite five minutes' 'work' of the year. That's because we're genuine fans of the show, we love *I'm a Celebrity*. And there's also the fact that we get to know before the rest of the country does – I mean, who doesn't like getting gossip before anyone else?

So back to the best recent example we mentioned. It was . . . drumroll please . . . Caitlyn Jenner. We were gobsmacked.

The producers couldn't believe our reactions; so much so that Richard said he wished he'd been filming it. But we were just in genuine, jaw-dropping shock that we'd got her.

You could make a strong case that she was the most globally famous person we've ever had on the show and, also, she was at a really interesting time in her life, which made putting her in the jungle all the more fascinating.

Obviously, she's a huge star thanks to Keeping Up with the Kardashians *and all the fanfare that goes with that, but, much, much more importantly, she was the first trans woman we've ever had on the show and, not just that, she is the most famous trans woman on the planet.*

That meant there would be conversations on the show about a subject that hadn't been covered in the previous 18 series, and that such an important issue would be covered on a mainstream, primetime programme. We both felt very proud to be a part of that.

And of course, aside from any of that, Caitlyn is just a fascinating person. She'd been an Olympic champion and,

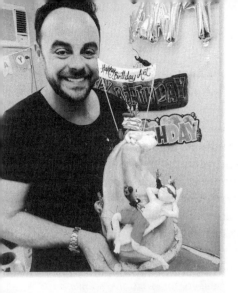

- Ant has won the Australian version of *e Great British Bake Off* five years running. -

despite her very pampered Hollywood lifestyle back home, she threw herself into every aspect of the show.

And she was also very open when it came to talking about her experiences – about how she'd worked through it with her family, about why and when she decided to transition and all the baggage that came with that. It was incredibly enlightening – a large section of the *I'm a Celebrity* audience were hearing about a lot of those issues in detail for the first time – and the same went for me and Ant.

That also meant that we had a few nerves about how we were going to approach the show, in terms of our links, because it's a sensitive, complex subject and you want to treat it with the enormous respect it deserves. We like to think we got it right, though.

And Caitlyn was incredible – and proof of the old rhyming maxim: 'The bigger the star, the nicer they are.'

I still can't believe we've almost made it to series 20. Who would have thought we'd have got this far when we went into camp in 2002 to crown Tony Blackburn as the first king of the jungle?

In our suits, don't forget.

How could we? I ruined a perfectly good pair of shoes.
But sitting here in our mid-forties, it also makes you realise how much has changed – these days, we both go out there with our families, but we were 27 when the show started and things weren't quite so civilised. We used to sleep a lot less and drink a lot more Australian lager, that's what I'm saying.

But these days, as well as our families, we still hang out with the same people, including our dynamic make-up and wardrobe duo, Claude and Toni. The main difference is that we're all about massages, yoga and amazing Australian smoothies.

'Amazing Australian smoothies' is our nickname for our drivers, Daryll and Shane. They're very handsome fellas.

And, of course, having our families out there is fantastic. The two of us had a moment last series, as we sat there with our grilled chicken salad and freshly squeezed orange juice, when we turned to each other and said, 'How the hell did we ever do this show on two hours' sleep?'

And, like anything we do, we have no idea how long it will go on, which makes us really appreciate it.

The year I didn't do it, I missed it so much. Not just the job and Dec and the show, but the whole experience – the place we stay in, the friends we've made over there – and, bloody hell, you realise winter is very long without doing I'm a Celebrity in the middle of it! I could not wait to get back there after a year away – and that made me value it all even more. How can you not be grateful for a job like that?

The year that Holly Willoughby stepped in, it was very strange for me to host a TV show with anyone but Ant by my side. Ant and I are both really good mates with Holly and she is a brilliant and accomplished presenter, but I had no real idea how she worked, nor she me, and we knew that, for the viewers, there was a curiosity factor to it all. People would be tuning in to see if we could pull it off and to pass judgement, which made it a nerve-racking prospect.

The thing about us two is that, for instance, I can interrupt Dec on a live TV show, and he can do the same to me, without disrupting the rhythm or the point of what we're saying, but that just comes naturally after three decades together.

Holly did a superb job and was fantastic to work with, and once we knew Ant wasn't going to be a part of that series, she was top of my list to host alongside me. At first, there was a lot of speculation as to who it would be, with people saying Stephen Mulhern or Phillip Schofield should get the job, but right from the very, very beginning there was no way I was going to host the show with another male. I didn't want to have another man standing on the same side that Ant stood. I didn't want it to appear that another guy was stepping in to take Ant's place, because they weren't. And because no one ever could.

We've talked about this before, but that's the first time I've heard you say all of that at once and it means the bloody world.

Reader, we are now hugging.

- We cover them up so the celebs can't see the time, not that anyone's EVER asked us that. -

- Show day. 5.30am, just before heading in to make-up. -

in? In Australia? This was NOT in the brochure. -

- Dec and his phone buddy. -

8

THE ROYAL FAMILY

This book might be all about our career in showbusiness and feature lots of celebrities, but if there's one thing we refuse to do, it's name-drop. A wise man once said to us, 'Never drop names.'

And that man was His Royal Highness, Prince Charles.

It's great advice that we'll try to follow in this chapter, which is all about us two spending time with different members of the royal family.

Absolutely.

Our first encounter with HRH came in 2001 when we interviewed him at Highgrove House, his family residence in Gloucestershire, for the 25th anniversary of The Prince's Trust. We were only 26 years old and it was incredibly nerve-racking, even if it did make our mams immensely proud. HRH asked us to become ambassadors for the charity, which we, obviously, immediately accepted. The work it does in helping young, vulnerable people get their lives back on track is enormously valuable. We've worked with them and supported them ever since; it's a charity we passionately believe in and have always been incredibly proud to be part of.

In 2006 our paths crossed again when we talked to Prince Charles, Prince William and Prince Harry together for an extremely rare joint TV interview, which included Prince William ribbing us about the PJ & Duncan years. Prince Charles even pretended he didn't know a single thing about our pop career, which made the joke even funnier.

Classic banter.

Then, ten years later we were asked if we would be interested in making a documentary about Charles creating The Prince's Trust and being the driving force behind it.

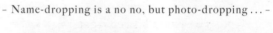
– Name-dropping is a no no, but photo-dropping . . . –

Naturally we said yes on the spot.

We asked Prince Charles if he would like to do I'm a Celebrity in return, but he politely declined. His loss.

The idea was that we would follow him around for the best part of the year, seeing first-hand the work he does and meeting people who have benefited from The Prince's Trust. And just to be clear, when I say, 'follow him around', I mean with a camera crew, not just us two hiding behind bushes and watching him everywhere he goes. That would be weird and creepy.

That meant that whenever HRH attended an event for the Trust, we'd turn up and he'd point at us and say stuff like, 'You two. Again. Is this legal?'

Of course, whenever we meet him, or any member of the royal family, it's normal to feel a bit nervous – and it's a different and altogether more serious kind of nerves than you get when you're hosting a live TV show.

We can't help but be conscious of what a significant figure he is. He's someone the entire population of this country, nay, the world—

Excellent use of 'nay'.

. . . has been aware of for as long as they can remember and we're no different, but he's an expert at putting people at ease. He seems to have a real appreciation of who he is and the impact he can have on others, and he works hard to make people relax, usually by being very charming and very funny.

And, over the years, we've got slightly less nervous every time we see him, especially when it was happening so frequently, as it did in the year we did the documentary. Slowly but surely, at various functions, we started to have fun with him. He's got a brilliant sense of humour and a twinkle in his eye. He understands and appreciates the effort people make when they meet him, although he says himself that he can't indulge everybody and everything. For instance, he's told us that everywhere he goes, people offer him food to try, but it would be impossible to eat it all, because he'd be the size of a house.

And when Prince Charles says 'the size of a house' you know that's a big house.

So, while we were following him, and filming the documentary, I took it upon myself to step in and try any food he was offered, just to help avoid any awkwardness. I could tell him what it was like, it would get him off the hook, plus the host gets their food eaten and I get a free lunch. Everyone's a winner. After a few functions I'd put on approximately half a stone and I could see him staring at me as I munched on some delicious Welsh rarebit (we were in Wales, obvs). HRH broke his gaze, slowly turned to Dec and asked, 'Is there anything he won't eat?' Then he turned back to me and regally bestowed a great honour upon me. 'I'm going to get a big spoon made for you. You can wear it on a chain around your neck. You can be my official taster.' I've never been so proud. Or so full.

Where is the royal spoon? I've never actually seen it.

Haven't received it yet. Probably still being made . . .

Probably.
     After a few months of seeing us semi-regularly (and realising he couldn't shake us off) he invited us to come and

stay at his residence in Scotland, where we would conduct the main interview for the documentary.

That invite completely blew our minds. No matter who you are or what you do, being invited to stay round at Prince Charles's should never feel normal. When you start taking a royal sleepover for granted, you've completely lost the plot.

Of course, we never referred to it as a 'royal sleepover' in front of HRH. And we never, ever said, 'I'm dead excited about the royal sleepover!' to each other in private.

Definitely didn't do that.

But once we'd established it wasn't a prank, we said yes and of course assumed that he'd put us in a different wing, as far away from him as possible.

We ventured up to Scotland and headed to Dumfries House in Ayrshire. As we made our way down the drive of this 2,000-acre estate, we looked at each other, unable to contain our excitement. We pulled up outside what was an 18th-century stately home to be met by two butlers who would be looking after us during our stay. That's right, kids, butlers! They took our luggage and led us through the entrance hall of this great mansion house to show us to our rooms. We climbed the main staircase and found our bedrooms at the top of the stairs at the end of a grand, emerald-green landing, with gold-framed portraits on the walls.

'Here's your room, Ant,' said my butler. 'Dec, you're opposite and Prince Charles is next door to you.'

'Sorry? He's what now?'

That's right. The three of us were on the same corridor, Dec next door to Prince Charles and me in the room opposite him.

And, yes, we've pitched it as a sitcom.

It was one of the most surreal moments of our lives. We must have been staring at this butler like he was speaking a different language. We looked at him, looked at each other and burst out laughing. My next question was obviously: 'Where is he now?'

'He's around,' replied the butler. 'He headed out to do a bit of gardening a little while ago.'

Our butlers unpacked our bags (I know!) and we settled into our rooms. We had a couple of hours to relax before we'd be attending a big, posh dinner downstairs that evening. I found a lovely fluffy robe on the back of the bathroom door and decided to slip into that for a bit. I was lying on my bed trying to make sense of it all and thought, 'I'll go over and see how Dec's getting on in his room.' I opened my bedroom door to cross the landing and who was coming up the stairs but the main man himself. Yep, HRH, in a body warmer, a flat cap, clutching a pair of secateurs. 'Oh hello,' he said. Pause. '. . . I've just been out front tending to the roses. Always better to do these things oneself, isn't it?'

Now, considering I've never tended to roses in my life and I'm standing there in a robe, in his house in the middle of the day, I decided to respond with, 'Oh absolutely, Your Royal Highness, these things are always better done oneself.'

Then there was that moment where neither of us knew what the hell to say next and may I remind you . . . I'M STOOD, IN A ROBE, IN HIS HOUSE, IN THE MIDDLE OF THE DAY. He smiled, I smiled, and then I did the only thing I could – I slowly backed into my room, closed the door and silently screamed into a pillow, leaving Prince Charles outside with his secateurs.

-'Stay at your house? Really? Yes please!' -

- Wallies with brollies in
blazing sunshine at The
Queen's 90th birthday. -

- Hosting the Prince's Trust Award.

- 'I might get my front room done out like this.' -

That night we attended the aforementioned posh dinner, where the guests included Rod Stewart and Elon Musk.

Together at last.

After dinner, we all retired to an anteroom. And if you're wondering, then, yes, 'retired to an anteroom' is definitely the poshest sentence in this book.

There was a bit of a party, bagpipes were played, people took a wee dram, there was a Highland fling and even a singsong, with Prince Charles giving his vocal cords a little run-out when he joined in with an a capella version of 'The Bonnie Lass o' Fyvie'.

We didn't join in because, as you'll remember from PJ & Duncan's trip to Indonesia, we don't sing a capella.

And then, at around 10.30pm, the host with the most called it a night.

And that was it, the end of the party. The party doesn't carry on when Prince Charles turns in. Cars arrived and took all the guests home. Except us, because, I don't know if we've mentioned it, but we were STAYING AT PRINCE CHARLES'S HOUSE.

We spent the next few hours – in my room (opposite Prince Charles's, don't know if we mentioned that) – reliving the evening, making each other laugh and then enthusiastically shushing each other, in case we woke up the future King of England.

The best bit is, he's a genuinely lovely man, and whenever we do anything for The Prince's Trust, he sends us a handwritten and usually very self-deprecating thank-you letter; it's always such a buzz when that one drops on the doormat.

Prince Charles loves writing letters. We spoke to Prince William and Prince Harry about it when we interviewed them, and they told us that he'll often sit up till late into the evening penning handwritten letters to people. They said that when they were away at school, he would write them letters and, when they read them, they could tell how late he'd stayed up, because the handwriting would gradually end up at more and more of an angle as he fell asleep at his desk.

When I got married in 2015, Ant got in touch with HRH. He politely declined the stag do (again, his loss) but he did send a handwritten letter to Ali and me, as well as a lovely wedding gift – a set of placemats that were all watercolours he'd painted himself.

You made a fortune with them on eBay, didn't you?

He's joking.

At the end of the year we'd spent with Charles for the documentary, I remember us going to a dinner for Prince's Trust ambassadors at Buckingham Palace. It was just before Christmas so that meant we'd just got back from Australia, which also meant we were seriously jet-lagged.

And Australian jet lag is the kind where you don't just feel tired, you also feel weird. Your teeth feel itchy, it's that kind of sensation. But anyway, we were ridiculously excited to be going to Buckingham Palace for the first time. For dinner. Our mams were also very excited and we promised to tell them all about it. We were shown into the main hall and Rod Stewart was there, he's always there (we're obviously on the same list as him). So we headed over to say hi to him and ask him if he'd seen Elon Musk recently, while keeping our eyes peeled for potential souvenirs. We'd heard a lot of stories about people liberating a memento when they go there.

'Liberating a memento' means nicking something – an ashtray, a toilet roll with a coat of arms, a full suit of armour, that kind of thing. And what struck us when we arrived was that there really wasn't that much there to nick, I mean liberate, either because they've got wise to the memento liberation brigade or because, if it's not nailed down, it's already been pinched by some opportunistic celebrity.

Oh, I've just remembered, George Clooney turned up.

Oi! Prince Charles told you never to drop names . . .

Sorry, but it's a big deal, he's a proper Hollywood superstar.
    Anyway, George Clooney turned up – and he was late, because, well, mainly because he's George Clooney, I'd imagine.

Now that is a man who could keep me waiting and I wouldn't mind.

Er, okayyyyyy.
    So George Clooney arrived and there was a lot of, 'Ooh, there's George Clooney' and, 'Look, it's George Clooney.' And that was just Ant and Rod Stewart. But once we'd had a look round, we noticed the only possible available trinket to nick, I mean liberate, was on the Christmas tree. As you can imagine, it was a Christmas tree bigger than any Christmas tree you've ever seen, and it had these baubles hanging from it in the shape of crowns. Brilliant. 'Nice baubles,' I said.

I half expected George Clooney to adjust his trousers and say, 'Thank you.'
    But he didn't. He was nowhere near us, because, well, mainly because he's George Clooney, I'd imagine.

I went over to have a closer look at the baubles and I took one off the tree to examine it. I'd had it in my hand for approximately 2.6 seconds, when one of the footmen appeared behind me and delicately but firmly whispered in my ear:

'Don't even think about it.'

I honestly just wanted a closer look. I wasn't going to 'liberate' it. I mean, think about it – to steal the decorations off the Christmas tree at Buckingham Palace, you'd have to have a huge pair of b—

Baubles?

Exactly.

It's a good job Ant didn't pinch the baubles because, a year later, we were asked to host coverage of The Queen's 90th birthday celebrations on ITV. If you didn't see it at the time, it was a concert featuring dozens of amazing musicians and actors.
And horses. Loads and loads of horses.

Hundreds of horses. Over 900 to be precise, from all around the world. It took place in a specially constructed arena in the grounds of Windsor Castle and we linked the whole evening together. There were star guest narrators, singers and musicians but mainly horses. People riding horses, standing on horses, jumping off horses, riding side-saddle on horses.

To be fair, at one point there were some cows and dogs involved. Her Majesty particularly enjoyed the cows – there was a great shot of her where you could lip-read her saying, 'Ooh, cows!'

It was amazing, not to mention pretty bizarre, standing on stage opposite the royal box with the whole Windsor family sat in there: The Queen, Prince Philip, Prince William, Kate Middleton, Prince Charles, The Duchess of Cornwall, Princess Beatrice and Princess Eugenie.

They really put the 'royal' into royal box . . .

And then there were the 6,000 other people in the arena, plus the millions watching at home and around the world. Now that's nerve-racking. It was an unforgettable experience, though, and thankfully we seemed to get through the whole show without any major hiccups. No one in a cape fell backwards down a set of stairs or anything like that, which is always a bonus.

At the end of the show, Her Majesty The Queen would be travelling from the royal box to the floor of the arena for a royal line-up, where she'd meet and thank the artists who had appeared. The plan was that we would wrap up the show on stage while she made her way down and, as soon as we were clear, we'd leg it round the back of the stage and into a waiting Range Rover. That car would then whisk us around the outside of the arena and, for the final part of the journey, we'd be picked up by a golf buggy, which would take us across the arena floor to join the end of the line-up, just in time to shake hands with HM The Queen.

And we were warned: 'Get your arses in gear, cos she's not hanging about.'

I think they said it in a more posh way than that, but you get the gist.

It wasn't as straightforward as just us two legging it to the Range Rover, though; we needed to bring Dame Shirley Bassey with us. She was the final performer of the night; then the national anthem would be played as the finale. The producer said, 'Make sure you get Dame Shirley off before they start the anthem, otherwise you'll have to stay put and you'll definitely miss the line-up.'

They also informed us that Dame Shirley, like most performers, liked to take her applause and a few bows, so we were told to make sure she was off or they'd just start the anthem with her on stage. If that happened, everyone would stand stock still, and we'd be stuck.

Sure enough, Dame Shirley finishes her performance and the arena erupts into rapturous applause. 'Thank you darlings,' she cries as she takes a well deserved bow, but behind the stage, a dark-green Range Rover is revving its engine, while the applause in the arena continues.

The clock was ticking while DSB was taking in her applause. We had by now edged onto the stage to catch her eye but she was oblivious to our nervous and eager stares. It was starting to look like we were destined to miss the line-up when, at the last second, DSB glanced in our direction. Bingo! We'd made eye contact. We frantically signalled to her that we had to go. 'Oops!' she said as she picked up the hem of her sparkly dress and trotted towards us as fast as her glittery heels would allow. Just as the three of us were leaving the stage, the orchestra struck up the national anthem. We had just made it off in time and we were on our way, but we were running late. We jumped into the waiting Range Rover and our driver kindly stepped on it.

We were raced round to the other side of the arena and then, as planned, were handed over to a waiting golf buggy. We could see the screens in the arena now and HM's face was beaming out as she made her way along the line-up, smiling and shaking hands. 'Oh God, she's on to Andrea Bocelli already,' I thought.

We helped Dame Shirley and her sparkly frock out of

the car (after 900 horses tramping through the gate, the ground was a total bog by this point) and got her onto the back of the six-seater buggy, facing outwards.

Ant and I jumped in the middle seats facing forwards.

'We all in?' asks the driver.

'Yep, let's go,' I reply.

He put his foot down. Hard. And suddenly, Dame Shirley goes flying forwards.

She was on her way to a face full of mud when our instincts must have kicked in. We both spun round and grabbed her by her sparkly dress and pulled her back into her seat.

But there was no time to pat ourselves on the back – not because our hands were still holding Dame Shirley's back (which they were) but because the race was still on to get to the line-up.

After a high-speed golf buggy journey, we arrived just as The Queen was coming towards the end of the row. She'd already shaken hands with the likes of Gary Barlow, James Blunt, Katherine Jenkins, Jim Carter, Alfie Boe, Dame Helen Mirren and Imelda Staunton, but she hadn't reached the very end. We'd done it. We'd wrapped the show, saved DSB from an unexpected face pack, made it to the line-up, and now we were going to shake hands with Her Majesty. We helped Dame Shirley into position and took the last two places ready to meet The Queen.

Then we looked down and noticed the red carpet HM was walking along. We realised that the people who'd arrived before us, your Blunts, your Barlows and your Stauntons, hadn't known there would be three (very) latecomers so had lined up accordingly and filled the red carpet. Basically, there was no red carpet left for us.

And, remember, the place was a muddy bog.

A few people managed to bunch up enough to get Dame Shirley in before the carpet ran out, so we just plonked ourselves on the end.

Basically, we ended up stuck in the mud next to the end of the red carpet.

Before the two of us could get the message 'move down, pass it on' going from person to person, Her Majesty had arrived at the end of the line. She shook hands with Dame Shirley, then peered across at us two, standing in our very own mini Glastonbury. She looked at us, then looked down at the ground. She looked back at us then took one more look at the mud underfoot and took a moment to work out what she was going to do.

Very sensibly, she thought better of it. No doubt thinking, 'I'm not getting my new birthday shoes dirty for these two,' she stayed on the red carpet but offered her hand – we dutifully leant across and shook fingertips.

Quite right too.

So what we got was the world's most awkward fingertip handshake with The Queen, coupled with the world's muddiest shoes.

They were even muddier than the ones we wore with our suits for the first *I'm a Celebrity* final – and that's muddy.

I suppose after the documentary in 2015 and The Queen's 90th in 2016, the third part of our royal trilogy came in 2017, when we were lucky enough to be awarded OBEs. It was one of those pinch-yourself moments, where you think, 'How did this happen? It feels like ten minutes ago we were doing the Junior Great North Run dressed as Teenage Ninja Turtles.' It just didn't feel real, we were gobsmacked.

– 'Thank you DSB! Now let's get in that golf buggy sharpish.' –

Backstage at the Queen's 90th
th James Blunt. He sang a song
bout how beautiful we were. –

– 'You've forgotten all the
protocol, haven't you?'
'Every last bit.' –

– 'Cheers! Here's
to photos taken
from the waist up
that don't reveal
muddy shoes!' –

It was such a huge honour and is definitely up there as one of the proudest moments of our 30 years together. To this day, I still can't really believe it happened.

When it came to the day of our investitures, we were so excited. My stomach was full of butterflies, because I just wanted it all to go off without a hitch. We also took time to remember to be 'in the present'; to take it all in and find time to actually enjoy it, because it was only going to happen once.

When it comes to handing out the OBEs, the responsibilities are shared by Prince Charles, Prince William, Princess Anne and HRH the Queen, and ahead of the big day we'd found out that Prince Charles would be awarding our OBEs to us. That helped us feel slightly more relaxed, because, although we were hardly BFFs, he's the member of the royal family we know best.

And, as his official taster, he's practically my boss.

We both invited our families down from Newcastle, as well as our managers and a few friends, and booked a private room upstairs at The Ivy restaurant in central London for lunch afterwards. For the ceremony itself, you get three guests each to take into the ballroom at Buckingham Palace, where it all takes place.

We got there and were taken to an anteroom (there's that word again . . .) with all the other people waiting to get honours. We were having a look around, checking out all the great art on the walls, seeing if there were any new mementos to liberate, when they came in and called our names. And this truly was a momentous day, ladies and gentlemen, as they called out, 'Donnelly, Declan' way before there was any mention of 'McPartlin, Anthony'. Yes, it was done alphabetically by SURNAME, folks. Victory at last!

I couldn't believe it, almost three decades of being Ant and Dec and when it came to the biggest moment of our entire careers – nay, lives – we were Dec and Ant. Not that it was that important, really. It wasn't a big deal to either of us.

Hallelujah! I was over the moon! Finally! It just goes to show, if you play the long game, you can come out on top in the end. In your FACE!

Ahem. Sorry, where were we? Ah yes. The other thing is that you get a very detailed briefing on the protocol before the big moment. You will be lined up near Prince Charles, they say, and once your name is called, you will take two steps forwards and you will turn to face him. Bow (from the neck – not the waist) then step forwards and HRH will attach your medal to a pre-attached pin on your lapel. You will chat and exchange pleasantries. When they are over, he will shake your hand. Finally, take two steps back, bow from the neck (not the waist, but you already know that) and then walk out of the room.

They made it crystal clear that it was very, very important to remember the protocol.

Reader, I forgot every single bit of it.

I basically walked forward and said a kind of 'Ooh hello' to Prince Charles, stuck out my hand to shake his and remembered I'd gotten it all arseways first! I collected myself, dropped my hand and tried to style it out, and said, 'Hello, Your Royal Highness.' I completely forgot all of the two steps forwards, bow from the neck stuff and just made a complete mess of the whole thing; the nerves and the excitement got to me. Prince Charles burst out laughing, which helped calm me down, and, fortunately, I still got my OBE.

The other thing you don't realise is that, after you've followed the protocol perfectly (thanks) and had your medal pinned onto your lapel, you exit the ballroom where someone extremely official-looking is waiting behind a table. They take it straight off your lapel and place it neatly into a presentation box, hand it to you and you're not supposed to really wear it again.

And there's a good reason for that.

I mean, we don't know what it is, but I'm sure there's a good reason for it.

You do, however, get given a smaller, replica version, which you can wear at official royal events (and food tastings), and you also get a pin badge, which you can wear anytime on your lapel. We normally wear those when we do something for The Prince's Trust.

We did take the real ones in their boxes to Manchester for some filming on the *Britain's Got Talent* auditions in 2018, though. David Walliams also got an OBE a couple of years ago and between the three of us we thought it would be enormous fun to tease Simon Cowell about him not having one. The minute we had that idea, well, we didn't like it, we loved it. It went like a dream and he was suitably green with envy. But there was a problem on the journey back from Manchester.

We flew back on Simon's private jet (la-di-da) and, when we went through security, we had to get our OBEs out of our hand luggage, so they didn't set off the metal detector. The trouble was, I had brought a delicious can of Fanta in my bag (in case they didn't do fizzy orange pop on private jets) and, unbeknownst to me, it had burst and soaked everything in there.

The medal is kept in this lovely posh velvety black box they give you, but now mine is forever stained with a delightful shade of Fanta orange.

Ant now has a fizzy OBE.

Every single one of our experiences with the royal family have been an enormous privilege. We feel so lucky that our job has given us the chance to meet and get to know some of them. It makes our mams very proud, which is always a good barometer, and we couldn't have dreamt of anything like this when we started out.

It's also something that makes you look back at the last three decades and consider how far we've come and how much we've been fortunate enough to achieve in our professional life.

And, of course, all of that just makes you want to celebrate, maybe raise a glass of something fizzy.

Fanta?

No thanks.

9

BRITAIN'S

GOT

TALENT

It might sound strange, but Britain's Got Talent *is another show we've done that has something in common with sm:tv. Not because we got the gig by sending a security guard with a briefcase round to Simon Cowell's house, but because the first time we were offered it, we said no. Yes, our uncanny gift for looking a TV gift horse in the mouth struck again.*

We'd seen the American version of *Britain's Got Talent*, which was, contain your surprise, called *America's Got Talent*. It was a big ratings hit for NBC and really very good. It had become the finished version of a show we'd helped to develop with Simon and the team at his then fairly new production company Syco, but the simple fact was, it didn't seem like the host had very much to do, so when we were approached to host the British version, we said, 'It's a no from us.' Thankfully, just as St Nigel of children's TV didn't give up in the late nineties, neither did ITV in 2007. They were very persistent and, eventually, like an egg being thrown at Simon Cowell by an irate violinist, we cracked.

But before we signed on the dotted line, we insisted on two things: a guarantee there would be a proper role in the show for the hosts and a commitment from Simon that he would be one of the judges. We thought that, after *Pop Idol*, the three of us being reunited would make good TV.

Plus, we'd have someone to make jokes about, which is always helpful.

One of the key things for us was making sure we had a connection with the acts, which didn't seem to be a big part of the American version. We knew from our Pop Idol experience that it was vital we got to hear from the talent before and after their performances, so we took the decision to stand at the side of the stage for every single audition — it was a great idea for the show.

It was, however, a terrible idea for our feet – they are absolutely killing us by the end of every session.

When it came to our role, we drew inspiration from one of our favourite childhood programmes, *The Muppet Show*. We loved the idea of 'the show behind the show' – all the chaos and mayhem going on backstage, with us two running around and helping the acts prepare, as well as making mischief with all the grown-ups who are out front.

And also because a lot of people say that we're a couple of muppets. It's a little joke that a lot of the crew make – it's funny because it's the total opposite of the truth, obviously.

Obviously.

And four years after Pop Idol had finished, it gave us the chance to get back on the talent show horse and, as always, try to be the voice of the audience. One of the lovely things about that is that we get to hear the acts' stories when the audience do (and before the judges), which means we're always rooting for them.

At the beginning of the first series of *BGT*, the producers put in a meeting every morning before the auditions started, so they could brief us on that day's acts. A couple of days in we asked to cancel the morning meeting, not because we wanted another half-hour in bed (which was a lovely bonus) but because we were 100 per cent sure we didn't want to know anything about the acts before we saw them. One of our favourite things about the annual audition process on *BGT* is that we genuinely don't know who's going to turn up at our side of the stage. We figured the audience at home didn't have a meeting with the producers before they watched the show (that would be a big meeting . . .), so we thought it didn't make sense for us to do it either.

- #TB to *SNTA*: A couple of Muppets with a couple of muppets. -

- *BGT* live shows. Occasionally,
we have to stop eating and do a
bit of TV presenting. -

- 'Hello and welcome to *Britain's Got
Talent*! If you need them, the toilets
are over there.'-

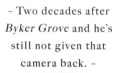

- Two decades after
Byker Grove and he's
still not given that
camera back. -

But before we meet a single act, every series we do something very important – film a sequence that ends with us saying the words, 'It's time to find out if Britain's Got Talent!' In TV terms they're called series openers (I bet you can't guess why). Sometimes they've involved me and Dec going to separate locations and, down the years, we've done them in some weird and wonderful places.

There was one that started with me stood on top of one of the pods on the London Eye. Physically outside of the pod, on top of it. It was an incredible view and so exciting. Apparently, they don't let many people do that, only a chosen few have ever experienced being up there. Where were you that year?

Whipsnade safari park. The traffic was so bad that it took hours to get there and, when we did finally arrive, it had gotten so late that the light was fading. Cameraman Andy set up the shot, but the soundman, Steve, was in a second car which was still stuck in traffic, so all we could do was film me, pretty much in the dark, mutely waving in front of an elephant.

They never used it in the show.

That was actually one of our alternative titles for this book, *Waving in Front of an Elephant*.

There was one where the producers asked if we would be prepared to ride down a zip wire and deliver the lines. We thought it didn't sound too difficult, so we said yes. The next thing we knew we were being driven to Wales to take on Velocity 2, the longest zip wire in Europe and the fastest zip wire in the world. It reaches speeds of over 100 miles per hour. After a health and safety briefing and several rehearsals of our lines to make sure we didn't muck it up, we were hooked onto the zip line. On the command of 'action', we were released and sped across the Penrhyn Quarry 500 feet in the air and, for once, we were word perfect on the first take. When we reached the bottom, we were over the moon . . . until we found out they'd forgotten to press record on the main cameras attached to us, which meant we ended up having to do it again. All in all, we had to do it about five times.

We also went white-water rafting in Milton Keynes and, another year, I was on a speedboat on the Thames, but I was on my own for that too. Where were you that day?

Probably taking a selfie with a penguin, knowing my luck.

When I was on the speedboat, we discovered there were restrictions that meant the maximum speed the boat could travel was 10 knots, which, as any nautical expert will tell you, is 'very bloody slowly'. The whole thing was being directed by Charlie Irwin, who is now the executive producer of *BGT* and is brilliant, but that day he didn't feel like we were getting the shot. He thought the boat wasn't quite delivering the dynamic opener we were looking for. Charlie knew how to fix it. He asked me to throw my arms in the air and shout 'Woo-hoo!' as if the boat were travelling at James Bond speed. He promised they could speed it up in the edit to make it look filmic and sexy. I love Charlie and I respect him a lot, but, on that occasion, I had to politely tell him to bugger off. Can you imagine? I would have looked like a grown man riding the teacups pretending he was on the rollercoaster.

By far the maddest one we ever did was in 2011, when we went up in a massive Union Jack hot-air balloon. It was, in theory, a very simple piece of filming – all we had to do was say something along the lines of, you guessed it, 'It's time to find out if Britain's Got Talent.'

We'd had the inevitable health and safety briefing and we

were due to take off, if that's the right term.

It's definitely not.

Fine, we were due to float up in the air at the crack of dawn in the middle of the countryside. There was only room for four people in the basket, which was us two, the producer and the pilot. Normally, our crew on BGT would consist of a producer, a runner, a sound recordist and a camera operator (we don't usually have a balloon pilot either).

The idea was that we'd be filmed from a camera that was in a helicopter, flying alongside us. So we all climbed in, with the producer having to crouch down so she was out of shot. We must have looked like a right load of basket cases. Literally.

The pilot was going to have to position himself as inconspicuously as possible in between me and Dec and was given one instruction: don't look into the camera. But once we started filming, it became apparent that the pilot was, well, how shall I put it? Far from camera shy. Every time we started to say our lines, his head would drift into the shot and he'd be grinning straight down the camera lens. We'd hear the producer's walkie-talkie on the floor crackle into life, going, 'Cut! Let's go again. Remember, don't look at the camera please.'

This happened several times. In the end, we convinced him to stop by telling him that he might be better off auditioning for the judges if he wanted to be on the show so badly.

Once we'd sorted that out, we were ready. The helicopter got into position, we cleared our throats, ran the lines in our heads, and we were good to go. But then, every time we started to speak, the pilot pulled the cord and blasted the burner flame. I'm not sure if he'd developed a grudge after we told him he wouldn't be starring in the shot, but the noise of the burner flame made everything we said utterly inaudible.

After another delicate chat with him, we finally got it filmed and told him we could turn back and head home to land.

And that's when he explained something crucial to us – you can't really 'steer' a hot-air balloon. Once it's up in the air, it just gets carried wherever the wind takes it and all you can really do is come down very slowly without any real idea where you'll end up.

Or, to put it another way, you have to crash-land.
Wherever you can.

As a general rule, balloon 'pilots' just look for an open piece of land and bring the thing down. We couldn't believe it – what kind of people turn up for work and basically make it all up as they go along?

Let's not dwell on that sentence, shall we?

Good point. We ended up just floating over the Home Counties looking for, essentially, a spare parking space for a hot-air balloon.

Eventually our prayers were answered. We spotted a field and there's no point in sugar-coating it, we crash-landed. And it was quite a bumpy one – I suppose the clue is in the title with a crash-landing. We narrowly missed the tops of some trees and eventually made it back onto terra firma somewhere in Kent, not that we knew where we were at the time. It was like landing in a time machine. Where are we? What year is it? Who's the President of the United States?

We'd only gone to Kent. Not 1963.

– 'What do you mean Ant still hasn't arrived
at Whipsnade Safari Park?' –

A hot-air balloon for the
opening, what could
possibly go wrong? –

– 'We all know this is never going
to be on telly, right fellas?'–

– Getting told to
'Zip it' in Wales. –

Shh. Once we'd ~~touched~~ *banged down, we all clambered out, dusted ourselves off and thanked our lucky stars we were still alive.*

While we were waiting and making small talk with the pilot ('Are you sure that's how you land balloons?' – that kind of thing) we saw two people come out of a house and make their way towards us. At first, we were worried they might be angry farmers, but, as they got closer, we realised it was – and this is going to sound weird – the *Strictly Come Dancing* dancers, Ola and James Jordan.

We couldn't believe it. I mean, what are the cha-cha-chances? They told us the President was Barack Obama and very kindly asked us in for a cup of tea, as if people crash-landed hot-air balloons next to their house on a daily basis.

It's the most light-entertainment end to a story ever.

So that's the series openers – what about the auditions? Well, as you know, we stand at the side of the stage and we've got a sweet little set-up going, by which I mean we are surrounded by sweets.

We eat A LOT of sweets – mainly Maltesers, Minstrels and giant chocolate buttons, fact fans.
We're there with our camera operator, Andy Clifford, and our sound recordist, Steve Bowden, who are both brilliant and have done every single series with us.

And on those audition days, well, when it comes to timekeeping, Simon Cowell makes Dec look like Britain's Most Punctual Man.

Thank you . . . I think.

We usually arrive at the theatre at about 2pm, ready to start auditions at 3pm. Before auditions begin, we might film some opening links for the show, often on a red carpet outside the theatre. Our arrivals sometimes involve different modes of transport – a horse and carriage, a motorbike and sidecar . . .

But thankfully no hot-air balloons.
And we also get to hang out with some of the judges at the auditions.

DAVID WALLIAMS: 'I love spending time with them on audition days. I remember going out with them in Manchester when we were doing some filming and there wasn't a single person who failed to clock them. They spoke to every single person who stopped them. I mean, I get recognised by people but not like they do. It was like a presidential walkabout.'

I hope he means presidential in a Barack Obama way, rather than a Donald Trump way.

A couple of hours after we arrive at the theatre , we focus on one of the key elements of any *BGT* audition day: waiting for Simon Cowell to turn up.

Once we've got started on that, we'll often film interviews with some of that day's acts, then have a bit of food, then get back to waiting for Simon.

SIMON COWELL: 'They used to have a real issue with me being late and it used to drive them nuts.'

We've still got a real issue with him being late and it still drives us nuts.

SIMON: 'We had to come up with some kind of compromise, which now means we work earlier.'

We've never come up with any sort of compromise, which now means we work later.

Nightmare, isn't it? Waiting for someone you know is going to be late, year after year after year?

I'm going to get on my tippy toes and rise above that.

Talking of size, it's a huge operation, a BGT audition day. There are around 270 crew members in the theatre and, on an average day, around 40 different acts will audition.

Sometimes there isn't enough time to finish all the chocolate we've got at the side of the stage.

And, of course, the talent comes in all styles, shapes and sizes. You get comedians and magicians, who have often honed their acts over years, desperately hoping this will be their big break. Then you get animal acts – they're often a winner, especially a good dog act. But whoever the performer is, we want to find out as much as we can about them before they go on: what are their hopes and dreams? Why are they here? And would they like some Minstrels or Maltesers?

We want to know how long they've been preparing, how they think it's going to go and, by the time they take to the stage, we're fully emotionally invested in these people – but we still have no idea whether they're any good or not. When they head out there, we have the same feeling they do: we're full of hope that they're going to be the winner of *Britain's Got Talent.*

And then they do their act and, of course, some of them absolutely nail it, some of them fall flat on their face, but the toughest acts to talk to afterwards are the ones who are just, well, OK. There's no big drama, no big story, but you know, and they know, that they haven't quite done enough.

But you don't have long to think about that, because the next act is walking towards you. That means it's time to focus on their hopes, their dreams and their attitude to circular chocolate treats.

And watching every act from the side of the stage means we literally have a different perspective on the talent. Literally. Sometimes you get an act that looks great sideways on, but then gets four buzzes – that's especially common with dance troupes. They can look great from the side, but then you watch it back, from the judges' and the audience's point of view, and they're all over the shop.

But without a doubt the best bit of any audition tour is seeing an act that just storms it – that blows away the judges and the audience. It is such a thrill to be there for those moments where the hairs stand up on the back of your neck and you feel the electricity in the theatre.

Another of our personal highlights is when an act gives as good as they get with the judges, just like Will Young did with Simon Cowell all those years ago.

To be fair to the judges, though, they do have to sit through A LOT of performances and they have watched some, ahem, unique stuff down the years. Do you remember the painting donkey?

Of course I remember the painting donkey. You never forget a painting donkey.

We were told by its owner that this donkey would be painting a picture. The donkey even arrived with its own entourage (which was three other donkeys) and we were sent to 'interview' the donkey.

Which meant the donkey was no longer the biggest ass in the story.

The interview didn't go brilliantly. Mainly because donkeys can't talk.

Thank you, Sir David Attenborough.

But despite the interview, we were still excited to see the painting donkey in action. That excitement turned out to be severely misguided. The donkey's 'act' consisted of the owner basically sticking a paintbrush in its mouth and it rubbing the brush on a craftily positioned canvas. We weren't overly impressed, and the judges weren't taken with it either.

I'll never forget Simon's response, which was, 'Bring him back when he can do a landscape.'

Animal acts can go one of two ways on *BGT*. Either they storm it, or they're a total disaster. Which leads me neatly to 2017 and the time the two of us and the judges brought our dogs to the theatre and we all took part in a dog yoga lesson.

Weird how we didn't get a BAFTA nomination that year . . .

My dog Rocky was fantastically well-behaved, as good as gold. Ant's dog Hurley was, well, how would you describe his approach to dog yoga, Ant?

He peed all over the stage.

We've both brought our dogs on the tour a fair bit down the years – they've kind of grown up on BGT – but that didn't stop my boy getting a bit carried away.

We all got on stage with the dog yoga instructor lady and our dogs and, in hindsight, we probably should have taken them out for a wee break before bringing them on stage, but Hurley saw the lights, heard the audience and wet himself, just like a lot of the animal acts do.

Like a lot of the human acts do, to be fair.

Let me tell you, it went on for ever. It is probably the longest dog wee in the history of British television. The producers looked back at the footage and timed it at 35 seconds. If you stop and count to 35 now, that is one very long wee.

As well as the instructor and her dog, Simon, David and Amanda had theirs on stage too. The instructor's dog smelt Hurley's wee, then became desperate itself, so quickly found the only receptacle it could.

David Walliams's shoe.

Nothing on *BGT* has ever made me laugh as much as I laughed that day.

They are the best judging panel on telly, though.

The dogs?

No, the humans. We love working with them.

They've all got different strengths: Alesha's the dance aficionado and she's got amazing energy when she loves an act; Amanda's a show-tune girl at heart, who is also a sucker for anything emotional; and Simon, despite being constantly late, still has an incredible ear.

Just one incredible ear? What about the other one?

OK, he's got two incredible ears. Now it sounds like I've got a thing about his incredible ears.

Simon knows exactly the right song for any singer and is a real populist, he knows what the public want. He's also got a new lease of life since he became a dad, so now he knows what kids want too – and, as a result, he's putting stuff through he would never have put through in years gone by.

And then there's David, who's obviously excellent at drawing tiny penises.

He's also been brilliant for the show; he's warm, funny and he brings out the best – and the worst – in Simon, which is often hilarious. And, of course, he's as disruptive as he was on The Ant and Dec Show 25 years ago.

In 2014, the Golden Buzzer was introduced and that added a huge new layer of excitement to the show. For an act to finish their performance and then be sent straight through to the live semi-finals meant there was so much more at stake at the auditions.

I also think the judges' Golden Buzzer choices tell you a lot about them. Simon often chooses a singer – but what you might not know is that he usually presses his Golden Buzzer on the first day of auditions. Partly because he's a very impatient man, but also because he just has to press it the minute he sees a singer who puts pound signs in his eyes.

They match his two incredible ears a treat, those eyes with pound signs . . .

Amanda will often go quite early too and usually for something that she is moved by – that could be the content of the act, or the performer's talent, anything that tugs at her heartstrings.

Alesha will almost always choose either a dance act or a comedian; that laugh of hers is infectious and, if you get her giggling, you're in with a good shout. And, as for David, he'll always hold out for something weird or wacky, or big and visual, or ideally all four. He's always the last one to hit his buzzer.

And then there's ours. I don't think we really have a 'type'; we go with something that turns our heads. We're also at a distinct disadvantage because of where we are situated. If we see an act we love, we have to run from the wings, across the stage, down the steps and then to the judges' desk to hit our Golden Buzzer – so if we love the same act as the judges, they'll get in there first. Invariably we end up going for acts that the judges wouldn't, and we pretty much both know when we see the right act; it's just a shared instinct we seem to have . . . so far.

Of course, we haven't always had the same judges. We started with Simon, Amanda and Piers Morgan, and then, in 2011, after series 4, Piers and Simon left the show. They were replaced by David Hasselhoff and Michael McIntyre, who joined Amanda for series 5. Michael was great on the show and very funny; and he couldn't help himself turning around in his chair to face the audience every time he gave a judgement – he loved playing to the crowd. Once a comedian, always a comedian. He had the audience in stitches, but the acts mainly saw his back when he was telling them what he thought of them.

And 'The Hoff'? Well, he was certainly different.
He was a lovely man and a bit crazy, which is always

fun. He was so eccentric that you just never knew who he would say yes and no to. But that wasn't the most frustrating thing about having David Hasselhoff on *BGT*, was it, Ant?

No. The most frustrating thing was that, on the audition tour, I kept getting booked into the hotel room next door to his. That in itself wasn't the issue, but he would regularly be up all night on the phone to his family or work colleagues in LA. Talking at the top of his voice. Loudly. After a long day of snacking on chocolate, I'd brush my teeth, put the light off and be dropping off to sleep, when I'd hear: 'Hey Marty, it's Hoff, I'm in Liverpool, how are you?' There were a few nights I had to bang on the wall to tell him to pipe down. I never saw that coming when I used to watch Knight Rider *in the 1980s in Newcastle.*

My abiding memory of that audition tour is Ant coming down for breakfast, looking absolutely knackered.
 I remember the first time it happened. I asked, 'How come you look so exhausted?'
 I wasn't quite expecting his reply . . .

I said, 'I've been up all night with David Hasselhoff.'

I nearly choked on my Sugar Puffs.

David and Michael only stayed for one series, which meant that a year later the show was looking for new judges to join Amanda on the panel. Obviously, they spoke to a lot of different people about the roles and, knowing how these things work, I imagine they had a lot of people in the mix at the same time. But there were two individuals they approached who we thought were a very, very peculiar choice to be the new judges on BGT.

- 'Where are we again?' -

- Talking cobblers on the famous cobbles. -

- Simon chatting to PJ on a PJ. -

- Five competition winners take their place on Simon's private jet. -

-No rest for the wicked: fitting in some extracurricular activities backstage in aid of a *Saturday Night Takeaway* EOSS. -

Us.

It happened in LA, where we'd stopped off on the way to Australia for *I'm a Celebrity*, and got a message to say Simon wanted to speak to us about the next series. Before we met him, we were expecting him to say he'd had some ideas for the judging panel and run them past us. And, in a way, that's exactly what happened.

He told us he had a great idea – he thought Dec and I should join the judging panel.

> SIMON: 'They absolutely hated it. And, of course, I loved it because they hated it so much. But at the same time, I couldn't do what they do. I could not talk to these contestants after they've done a terrible audition and pick up the pieces. I think that's much tougher than what we do.'

Can you imagine? Simon at the side of the stage, talking to acts after they'd been judged by us two . . .

We talked about Simon's offer on the flight over to Australia, then slept on it – the idea, not the flight, although we did also sleep on the plane; it's a long journey and they give you special pyjamas.

But, after much deliberation, we decided against becoming judges. We thought we belonged firmly on the side of the acts, at the side of the stage, and that us joining the panel would bring unwanted pressure. Plus, we thought that because we know how hard all the acts work, we'd want to put every single one of them through!

We rang Simon to give him the news. We thought we might have a battle on our hands to persuade him that it wasn't for us at that time. We thanked him for the offer, told him our reasons and then listened to his response, which was:

'Oh, OK then, I'll get someone else.'

That was it. No 'Please reconsider', no 'Come on, it'll be brilliant'. Just 'OK then, bye', basically.

There are times when we envy the judges, though, especially on the audition tour. They get a lovely big judges' room, full of delicious food; they get lots of breaks, and they get to sit down all day in a nice comfy chair.

Whereas we get crisps and chocolate and two 20-minute breaks a day.

We made the wrong decision, didn't we?

Totally.

Another friendship we developed on BGT was with Stephen Mulhern. We knew him loosely before we all started on the show, but we began to work more closely with him, and we really clicked. As we said when we were talking about Takeaway, he makes us crease up laughing on a regular basis and, throughout all the years of the show, he has never, not once, missed a trick to get us involved in some daft game for Britain's Got More Talent.

> STEPHEN MULHERN: 'I think my favourite was when Dec had just become a dad. We came up with a game to test how good he was at changing nappies. We got hold of some adult diapers and then Dec had to use Ant to demonstrate how to change a nappy. Ant told me they wouldn't have let anyone else on TV do that with them, which meant a lot ... even if he was wearing an adult diaper when he said it.'

For the record, I did an <u>excellent</u> job of putting on that nappy.

You must be so proud . . .

Whenever we were in the theatre, we would walk around any corner and there they were: Stephen, a bunch of cameras and a brilliantly cheeky game. He's a little ray of sunshine on those long days in the theatre, though. And by 'little ray of sunshine' we mean 'a pain in the arse'.

Only joking, Stevie, we love you really. He is a big miss around the theatres now that *Britain's Got More Talent* has come to an end.

Someone else we've spent a lot of time in theatres with is Simon – and not just when he's trying to persuade us to join the judging panel and then not being remotely bothered when we say no. Over the years, we often catch up with Simon in LA too, which is where he spends a lot of his time. There was one dinner I remember when he was particularly interested in how our racehorse was getting on.

A couple of years earlier, we'd got friendly with a few people who owned horses and decided it would be a fun thing to get involved with. A trainer called James Fanshawe found us a horse we could invest in. It was called Primeval and it did really well. It raced at Kempton, Goodwood and Ascot, winning a few times – and it even qualified to run at Royal Ascot.

After a few years of racing, Primeval was about to retire and we decided we'd like to invest in a new horse, so we were looking for other people to join us. We knew Simon was a big racing fan, so we mentioned it to him, and he liked the sound of it.

We agreed between the three of us that we'd all have a think about a good name for the horse, so me and Dec came up with some options and called up Simon. Right from the off, he told us he had a great name, one he was really excited about. We thought, 'Brilliant, Simon's named the biggest pop groups in history, he's a branding genius, this is going to be amazing.' And then he hit us with it:

'I think we should call the horse Simon.'

And he was deadly serious.
Not only is it a very weird name for a horse, but it also didn't really include us two. It's classic Simon Cowell, really.

In the end, we called it 'It's A Yes From Me'. Still pretty Simon-centric, but it was a name that tickled us all. I think I actually suggested it – so in the end, for Simon, it was a yes from him for 'It's A Yes From Me'.

Once we had the name, next up we had to agree on the colour of the silks (the jockey's uniform). Meanwhile, the trainer trained the horse and it turned out to be . . . what's the word I'm looking for?

Disastrous.
It was the worst racehorse in history. In fact, you could have taken it to the Trading Standards Authority for calling it a racehorse. It was just a horse. It never really got to grips with the race side of things.

It had a lovely upbeat personality, though; it never had a long face, which spoiled a lot of potential jokes.

After it became clear it wasn't going to win the Epsom Derby, or even outrun a toddler, we knew the whole thing had been

– With Primeval: 'Why the long face?'

'I've just got a big forehead, OK?' –

– Filming in Hyde Park 2020 and finding ourselves up a creek without a paddle. –

– BGT audition days are just one big laugh from start to finish. –

a waste of time. The next time we saw Simon was at the live semi-finals, and he said, 'We need to talk about It's A Yes From Me.' We said, 'It's a no from us,' and made a sharp exit.

In our defence, we are very busy on the days of the live shows.

One of the things we always make sure we do when we get to those live studio shows of *BGT* is have a good chat with the contestants to try to help calm their nerves and put them at ease, especially with kids who are performing.

> DAVID: 'When you ask any visitor to the *BGT* studio who they want to meet, the answer is always "Ant and Dec". And they're just so unbelievably generous with their time. They're working really hard, but they've always got time to talk to everyone and make them feel special, and everyone comes away from meeting them smiling and having had a great experience.'

I'm starting to think we should hire David Walliams as our agent . . .

The studio is a madhouse on those days: you've got dance acts doing backflips down corridors, you can hear vocal warm-ups from singers' dressing rooms, the judges are coming and going with their entourages – it's a hive of colourful and bizarre activity and, if they're not used to it, it can be quite daunting for the acts.

It can also be intimidating once the show starts, with a full audience, the judges and all the cameras and lights, so we try to give everyone the best possible chance to do well on the show.

And if that gives us the chance to avoid someone we've persuaded to invest in a racehorse, then all the better.

Of course, things don't always go according to plan in the studio – probably the best example of that came in the 2013 live shows, when Simon got egged.

It happened slap-bang in the middle of a performance from opera duo Richard and Adam. They had a line-up of backing singers and classical musicians behind them on stage and suddenly, out of nowhere, a woman who was posing as one of the violinists came to the front of the stage armed with a box of eggs and started pelting Simon with them.

It's not uncommon for an act to make changes in between the rehearsals in the afternoon and the live show in the evening, but this seemed like quite a big rethink for an opera duo, adding half a dozen flying eggs to their act.

Once we got word in our earpiece that this wasn't part of the performance and it was in fact an intruder, we legged it back up onto the stage, ready to restore some order and try to explain what was going on.

At first, we were all a bit shocked, because obviously it could have been a lot more serious – but when we realised they were only eggs and that everyone was OK, well, you start to see the funny side. Shame she missed him with most of them. I remember thinking, 'I wonder what Simon's going to make of that?'

My money was on an omelette.

But whatever happens, *BGT* is always an event, it always has been – and it has an impact around the world, not just here.

Years ago, I was on holiday in Dubai and I went to get a burger from a shopping mall next to the hotel. When I'm abroad, no one has a clue who I am, so I was looking forward to a nice quiet burger and a sit-down.

I'm sat there, tucking into my Quarter Pounder with cheese, when a local boy comes over to me and says, 'It's you, isn't it?' pointing at me excitedly. He asked for a selfie, so we did a selfie and then he said, 'I can't believe I got a selfie with Susan Boyle Boy! Thank you, Susan Boyle Boy!'

It took me a moment to put two and two together, but I worked out that he'd obviously seen Susan's audition on YouTube. That clip has had hundreds of millions of views and there's a fairly memorable moment in it where I turn to camera and say, 'You didn't expect that, did you?'

I mean, it's always nice to meet a fan, but 'Susan Boyle Boy' is not my favourite nickname.

Come on, lighten up, Susan Boyle Boy.

Being part of a show that's gone so global has been a real buzz for us and, naturally, it has its advantages. For example, whenever we go through US Immigration, it's a big help. As anyone who's done that knows, it can be one of the most intimidating experiences of your life – it's like being interrogated by Jack Bauer in *24*.

But whenever we go through, the conversation goes like this:

Them: Occupation?

Me: TV host.

Them: Oh yeah? Anything I'd know?

Me: You know you guys have got *America's Got Talent*? Well, I host the British version, *Britain's Got Talent*.

Them: So you know Simon Cowell?

Me: Yeah, I know Simon Cowell. He's a good friend of mine.

Them: Come right through, sir. Welcome to America. You have a great day now.

I mean, I'm not saying everyone should try it, but it works for us – so thanks, Simon.

But it was on one of those trips to America, in 2012, where we had to have a serious conversation with Simon. The previous series of BGT had been especially tricky for us two. The audition days had been very long, which in itself we don't mind, but after filming interviews and interacting with every single act, as well as making jokes, giving reactions and everything else we always do, we found that when the show went out on TV, we hardly seemed to feature in it at all.

We began to feel that we were wasting our time doing the auditions because all the footage of the work we were doing was ending up on the cutting-room floor. And, what's more, with Saturday Night Takeaway about to come back into our schedule, we could have been putting our efforts into that in January, when the auditions happen. The experience left us feeling like we were being sidelined.

We'd been to see the bosses at ITV and told them we were strongly considering leaving *BGT*.

At that stage, it felt like it may as well have been anyone hosting the show and we said that when our current contract expired, we thought it was time to move on.

This isn't something we're in the habit of doing and they aren't easy conversations to have, but we felt like honesty was the best policy.

I remember waking up in Birmingham on the last day of the 2012 tour, opening my curtains and thinking, 'Well, this is the last time I'll be doing this.'

Taking part in a BGT audition tour, not opening a pair of curtains.

I'll never stop opening curtains. Never.

The ITV bosses told Simon about the conversation we'd had with them and he asked to meet. We agreed to catch up with him in LA to talk about it. We've always had a lot of respect for him and, whatever happened, we wanted to talk to him face to face.

The three of us went to a restaurant in West Hollywood called Ceconni's and we sat outside, partly so we could soak up the glorious Californian sunshine, but mainly so Simon could smoke.

And it's worth mentioning that Simon was only one minute late for that meeting, which for him is the equivalent of being three days early. The three of us sat down and me and Ant went either side of him, so we could do the full pincer movement.

He started by saying how he'd thought the last series was amazing, how well it had gone, how pleased he was with the talent, and then he asked us how it had been from our side.

And then we let him have it with both barrels.

We told him everything – that we weren't being used, that we could be doing other stuff, that maybe someone else should take over. To be fair to Simon, he sat there, took it all and listened intently for four, maybe five cigarettes.

And then he made a promise to us: that things would change and that we'd never feel like that again. He desperately wanted us to stay and we told him we'd do the next series and see how it went – and, to be fair to him, he was as good as his word, things did change.

SIMON: 'If they're p****d off, they'll tell me to my face. And there's no drama. There's no entourage. If they've got something to say, they say it themselves, which I respect.

> But we've worked together for nearly 20 years and I don't
> think we've ever really had a falling-out, which is incredible
> if you think about it.'

After we'd cleared the air, the three of us had a lovely meal. I seem to remember a lot of smoked food.

No, no, Simon just smoked a lot near our food.

Oh yeah.

At the end of the evening, Simon offered us a lift back to our hotel in his chauffeur-driven Rolls-Royce. We were only staying around the corner, but apparently nobody walks anywhere in LA; plus, we'd never been in a Rolls-Royce before, so we said yes, settled the bill and made our way to the car.

The driver opened the back door on the passenger side for Simon, who got in first, followed by me on the driver's side. Simon and I were sat comfortably in the two back seats – the only two back seats – when Dec clambered in and adopted this weird half-standing, half-crouched position facing Simon, while fiddling around with his hands behind his back. After a couple of seconds of stunned disbelief, Simon said, 'What the bloody hell are you doing, Dec?'

I said, 'I'm looking for the seat.'

For reasons that still escape me to this day, Dec thought there was a flip-down seat in the back of a Rolls-Royce, like you get in a black cab.

Well, I'd never been in a Rolls-Royce before.

Neither had I, but I didn't get it mixed up with a black cab.

Eventually, after Simon and I had stopped laughing, which took about ten minutes, Dec got in the front passenger seat. The big boys in the back had a nice chat while Dec strained to hear us.

Yeah, yeah, can we just get on to the next chapter please?

All right, no need to flip out.

I'm not flipping out.

Just like the seat in a Rolls-Royce then.

10

DNA

JOURNEY

Someone wise once said, 'It's not about the destination, it's about the journey.'

Who was that?

I don't actually know. I've googled it and all I found was a car sticker and two fridge magnets.

Not the best start to a chapter then, is it?

It was fine till you stuck your beak in asking who said it. Can we just crack on?

Fine.

Back in 2012, we had an interesting phone call from a man called Alistair Moffat. He's a historian who happens to be the uncle of our writer, Andy Milligan. Alistair is also an intelligent and esteemed author who's written countless books and is a former Rector of St Andrews University.

And Andy has spent the last 15 years writing jokes about turkey testicles for us two.
In 2007, we made a TV show with Alistair about the history of Tyneside, based on one of his books, and we stayed in touch. In
that 2012 phone call, Alistair told us he'd set up a DNA business for people who were interested in finding out more about their ancestry. He explained there was a lack of samples being provided in the Northeast and asked if we would do a test and publish the results in the local paper, to encourage more people in the region
to come forward.

We said yes, partly because we're very fond of Alistair and we have a lot of respect for him, but mainly because all we had to do was spit in a test tube and send the saliva off for analysis.

A few weeks later, Alistair came back to us and said the results were fascinating. So fascinating, in fact, that he wanted to meet up and talk to us face to face. At the meeting, he wouldn't tell us why, but he revealed that he thought the results had the scope for more than local news – he thought they could be a TV show, a TV show where the two of us traced our ancestry.

Like everything in television, the whole thing took a few years, but we started talking to Siobhan Greene, who at the time was the controller of ITV Entertainment and is someone we've had a working relationship with for almost two decades. You may remember her from earlier chapters, such as the one on Saturday Night Takeaway.

Siobhan was immediately interested in the idea and eventually, almost five years after that first bit of spittle, we started making what became *Ant and Dec's DNA Journey* for ITV.

We didn't know it at the time, but it would turn out to be one of the most important things we've ever done.

For a start, the way we made the show was the polar opposite of the way we work on any of our other shows. Normally (with the exception of Britain's Got Talent *auditions) we know absolutely every inch of everything that's going to happen and we are as prepared as we can possibly be, but on DNA it was vital that we were kept in the dark as much as possible. And that meant putting our trust in other people.*

– Playing hide and seek (Ant's behind the drystone wall).
So embarrassing that they caught that on camera. –

– Another exclusive shot of us two
before we head into make-up. –

– A'n'D talk DNA on
stage at BAFTA. –

While Ant, with his love of the unpredictable (not to mention the fact he's a huge history buff), jumped in with both feet, the lack of control was something that made me feel uncomfortable at first.

Clearly, it was vital we didn't know what was going to happen, so that we could capture our genuine reactions when we got information about our families that we'd never heard before, but it still took me a long time to relax and let go.

And, of course, it wasn't just the lack of control that made it a leap of faith — it was also because it was a different genre of TV from the one we usually do. Normally, the shows we host are about other people, but this was very much about Ant and Dec.

We had a lovely team to work with, led by Iain Thompson, aka 'Thompy', our producer/director, alongside a smaller crew than we're used to, which we really enjoyed.

And that's important, because the older we get, the more work is about finding the enjoyment in the process as well as the end product. We want to do things we enjoy and, if we are having fun during the making, we hope that comes over on screen.

I went into it with hardly any knowledge of my family beyond the last couple of generations, so it was a real journey into the unknown. I was particularly in the dark when it came to the paternal side of my family, because for a long time I hardly knew my dad. But from the second day of filming, in the Tyneside Irish Centre, when I was told that my great-grandfather, Peter McPartlin, won the Military Medal in the Battle of the Somme, I realised this was going to fill in so many of the huge blanks in my family history. Talking about my granddad and my great-granddad and putting faces to names and timelines and family trees meant the world to me.

The way the show worked fascinated us too. It was so different from anything we'd done on TV. Or in life, for that matter. We didn't know what was going to happen or where we were going to go until we got a 'DNA Alert' – these were texts we received and, every time we got one, it would be the first clue in the hunt for our next relative, or the next significant place connected to our ancestry. We literally had no idea where this journey would take us, or what we'd find when we got there.

And it was a journey that took us all around the world, both in terms of knowledge and air miles. We found out things about our ancestry that took in places like Turkey, Iraq and Syria, and, from starting out in Newcastle, we travelled to Ireland, Northern Ireland, New York, Connecticut and Philadelphia and went back thousands of years. On my maternal side, we traced my ancestors back to 6300 years BC, to the site of an 'archaeological find of historical importance'.

And then there was Dec's family line, which went back to 2500 BC, to the Beaker folk.

They were named after a pot.

And were known for making porridge.

It wasn't a competition.

Of course not.

Although let's not forget that I am also descended from a High King of Ireland. So, if it was a competition, I would have won.

But it wasn't a competition.

No, it wasn't.

We were both really, really struck by how incredibly

emotional we found the whole experience – we've never cried so much on telly in our lives.

And, despite all my reservations about the process, it became quite a healthy exercise, to relinquish control and show vulnerability when you're not used to either of those things. *What we both loved, though, was just being filmed, chatting, usually in the back of the car, in a way we do when we're together and in a way we have done all our lives. I think people get a pretty realistic sense of who we are and what we're like from watching us on TV, but this was a much closer reflection of what we're like in private. And it was all very loose and relaxed, because after three decades we're not just completely at ease with each other, but also on camera, mainly because we've spent two thirds of our lives on the telly.*

That also meant that, as well as the kind of genuine moments of friendship, teasing each other, laughing together, we also had moments of intimacy and emotion, which, largely, is something new for us to show on TV.

And the public's reaction to that was something so special. We always place such stock in our audience, and this was us showing them a completely new side of ourselves. I think the raw emotion of it appealed to them.

And, even better, a lot of people said it encouraged them to look into their own DNA, their own family tree, their own history, and that was something we were immensely proud of.

We also met some incredible family members, people we never would have encountered without this show.

And when you meet those family members, you feel an immediate kinship with them – it's a difficult sensation to describe, but there's an instant connection, you can feel the family bond you have, which is something very special.

One of the relatives who stuck with me was a singer called Mary McPartlin. We met her when we went to Drumkeeran (a village in Ireland) and walked into a pub full of people who all shared my DNA. Mary performed a beautiful rendition of an old Irish folk song called 'Slieve Gallion Braes'.

It was a song that was played at my dad's funeral, so I found it incredibly moving and so poignant. I had no idea Mary was going to sing it and it absolutely floored me. It was a special moment.

Sadly, Mary passed away recently. She was a lovely woman who I stayed in touch with after filming and I still listen to recordings of her folk music.

One of my relatives who surprised me the most was a lady called Dixie Carter, a hugely successful American businesswoman who for a long time was involved in the wrestling industry. I'm still in touch with Dixie and, when she was on a European vacation (that's American for 'holiday') last year, she came to *Britain's Got Talent*. It was so lovely to see her again and you never lose that feeling of family connection.

There was also Greg and Meg, relatives of mine in Connecticut, who were lovely and . . . what's the word I'm looking for?

Billionaires.

That's it. I've emailed them a few times, but I've not heard anything back yet. Either I've got the wrong email address, or they want nothing to do with me.

I know which one my money's on.

Making that show was full of wonderful moments,

'My family are here; the
signs are everywhere.' –

ousin Dixie. She too has a
e and hair – such a strong
family resemblance. –

– Another calendar shoot:
'Hello Mr February!' –

– So glad I didn't go to Specsavers. –

though. One of the most memorable happened off camera, so it didn't make the show, but it was when we arrived in Drumkeeran. We walked past a sign that said 'McPartlan Opticians'. Outside of my own family, it was the first time I'd ever seen my surname written down anywhere. Even though it had a slightly different spelling, it felt so special, like the key to a whole world I'd always known existed, but never knew how to access. It was so much more than a sign on a shop to me, and it made me more certain than ever that this was going to be something remarkable.

I remember on the way to Drumkeeran, we stopped at a small village called Drumshanbo for some lunch. And, pretty quickly, word got out that we were there and as we were looking out of the window more and more people kept arriving. By the time we came out, it felt like the whole village was there – we were even passed babies to have photographs taken with.

There was a warmth in the welcome that felt specific to Ireland and we couldn't leave until we'd signed every autograph and done every selfie; it was overwhelming and joyous all at the same time. It felt like people loved that we were visiting their village as part of a journey towards finding out about ourselves and our history.

I think this is also the kind of show we could only have done at the age we are and the point we're at in our lives. No one wants to watch the 22-year-old founders of Ant and Dec Productions go on this kind of journey – they hadn't lived enough life and didn't have enough perspective on the world. But, in a strange way, this experience came at exactly the right time for us.

It also turned out to be the best way for us to talk about the events of the last few years, with the problems I'd had and the break I took from television. This show was a place where both of us could be honest about what happened and the effect it had on our relationship. By the end of making DNA, our partnership was so much stronger than it had been at the beginning, because so much had happened to us both. I'd gone through rehab and a divorce and Dec had become a dad for the first time. These are seminal points in your life, huge moments that, especially in my case, could have gone either way.

There were times in my recovery when I wasn't sure if I'd work again, or if I'd get to work with Dec, if we'd ever get to be Ant and Dec again. That sounds crazy now, but at the time it weighed heavily on my mind, because, at first, my prime focus had to be on getting myself well.

Looking back, when we went into *DNA*, our relationship wasn't where it should have been. We were on autopilot, working too hard and taking each other for granted, but Ant's break forced us both to evaluate everything, almost with the perspective of an outsider.

And Ant's right, there was a real chance that we were never going to work together again. Not knowing if Ant and Dec would continue was very scary for us both. Since 1990, we've made every decision together, for the sake of Ant and Dec. Every discussion we've ever had has been, 'What are we going to do? What's best for us?' And now, suddenly, we had to think about ourselves as individuals: 'What do I want to do? What's best for me?' That felt like such an alien mindset to adopt. And it was very frightening.

It was something we really took our time over. We both spoke to lots of people, friends and family, and we both individually came to the conclusion that we wanted to

- On top of Slieve Gallion in Northern Ireland, excited about a trip to the Big Apple. -

- Dec with his American family in the good old US of Stateside. -

- At the United Nations: 'All these empty seats remind me of our pop star days.' -

keep working together. A break helped us realise how much we love what we do and, ultimately, how much we love each other.

And it actually made us stronger. We rediscovered what made us happiest and that we still shared so many of the same goals and ambitions.

It was a reset and a huge reminder of everything that we hold so dear about our partnership. And, of course, how incredibly lucky we are to do what we do. Our job is to have fun and we are both incredibly grateful for that.

The show really is a story of two halves – before and after what happened. At one point, it was suggested that we might want to just ignore the two-year gap in filming, but we were never comfortable with that. What happened was so widely publicised, this was a chance for us both to front up and take ownership of the situation. It just so happened that this documentary chronicled that period, so we took the opportunity to tell the story in our own words.

And we got to do that with a crew we trusted and in interviews where we could both be completely and brutally honest about what had happened and how it made us both feel.

And we're both different people now; we're not the same Ant and Dec who started making DNA. There was a lot of soul-searching done during the two years it took to make the programme. We're stronger and happier than we were, thanks in no small part to those huge changes in our lives.

Becoming a dad has completely transformed me. At first, like all expectant parents, I didn't truly understand how much it was going to change me. I just thought, 'It's another little person coming to live in the house.'

Another little person. Nice for you not to be the only one . . .

That's not what I meant.

But it opened up a whole other side to me, a side I didn't know existed. I felt a love that I didn't realise it was possible to feel. Everything I do, every day, is for my daughter now. And, of course, going on my _DNA Journey_ was a huge part of that – me finding out where I came from is something she will always have and, hopefully, growing up, it will give her a clear sense of who she is and where she's from.

Doing the show ended up being for her.

One of the biggest things the show did for me was that it gave me the chance to reconnect with my dad. In 2017, we hadn't seen or spoken to each other for ten years and my relationship with him didn't really exist.

But once I started finding out stuff about the paternal side of my family, it felt like the right time to contact him. When a parent leaves and you have a distant, or sometimes non-existent relationship, it means that when you do see them, you can struggle to find common ground, but now I had a whole family history to tell him about, like my great-grandfather, the war hero.

And when we did meet up, we bonded over all of that immediately. He loves history too, so it gave us an immediate and brand-new connection. He even remembered some of the details about Peter McPartlin. My dad recalled times as a kid when he would sit on his knee and his granddad would tell him all about having a bullet hole in his arm – that was from the Somme, which DNA had taught me all about.

Me and my dad's relationship blossomed from there and it's gone from strength to strength ever since. Without the show, that might never have happened.

I lost my dad in 2011 and finding out about my ancestry wasn't just important for my daughter, but also for the rest of my family. My dad used to tell us stories and we'd ask questions, but, like any family, there was only so much you could ever find out, so *DNA* gave me the chance to fill in some of the gaps – and, of course,
go further into our family history than ever before.

It was incredible for me and Ant to make a show with such purpose – normally, the work we do (and love) is about talent-show winners, turkey testicles or giving away places on the plane, but this was such a rich and complex story, it was unlike anything else we'd ever done.

And, like all the best stories, it had an ending that no one, including us, saw coming.

If you didn't see the documentary or can't remember it, then, spoiler alert, what we discovered was that we are related. We share the S660 DNA marker, which makes us DNA cousins – we are both related to a Viking-era warrior from Ireland, who lived around AD 790.

Good old great-granddad, the Unknown Viking Warrior. Love that guy.

And, going back to that first phone call about the local paper from Alistair, that's what he meant, that's why he thought this was a story worth telling on a bigger canvas, and now we've told that story, we think he was right.

We keep saying it in this book, but we mean it every time – this felt like the most important TV show we'd ever made. It changed our lives and it changed our friendship, and all for the better.

And we now have actual scientific proof that we are Vikings.

Well, I'm not sure about that.

Button it.
   Cousin Ant.

- 'Sure, we're about to get in that helicopter, no big deal.' -

- A banner that says, 'We come Cou n Dec'. Must be an American thing. -

- In Philadelphia, with the Rocky statue and its slightly-too-long-arms. -

FIVE
QUESTIONS

Before we get to the end of the book, where we tell you how much we've grown and developed as people over the last 30 years, we're going to ask each other five random questions all about the kind of everyday stuff that only best mates know about each other.

Why? Well, because we liked the idea and it's our book, OK?

QUESTION 1: Tell me about the start of your working day.

Well, our driver Joe arrives at my house to pick me up, rings on the Donnelly doorbell and then it usually takes a little while before I get in the car.

'A little while'?
    You're 15 minutes late every time – you're reliably unreliable. It's been happening for years.
    What do you actually do during those 15 minutes? I've always wanted to know.

Firstly, I'd like to point out that science has proved that people who are late are more successful and live longer. It's in my DNA. I'm surprised you're not late too, because we're cousins.

You're even keeping me waiting for the answer to this question. Why. Are. You. Always. Late?

I try to be on time, I really do. I don't know how it happens. I often think, 'Oh, I'm five minutes early today and I'm ready! I've even got time to do a little job.' Then that little job takes ten minutes and then, of course, I have to brush my teeth.

What?

It's always the very last thing I do before I leave the house. I've got an app on my phone that's connected to my electric toothbrush and it makes sure I brush for exactly two minutes, so once I notice I'm late, I'm always going to be a further two minutes late, because I've got to brush my teeth. I've got to see it through.

Why don't you just brush your teeth earlier?

It wouldn't feel right.

You're not doing yourself any favours here.

OK then Ant McPunctual, tell me about the start of your working day.

I get ready ON TIME, I brush my teeth IN GOOD TIME and then I have a little ritual I always start the day with.

Oh yeah, what's that?

I sit and stare out of my window, waiting for this bloke who keeps me waiting for 15 minutes every day because he's brushing his teeth via an app on his bloody phone.

QUESTION 2: What's the last text we sent each other?

OK, let's have a look. This is the last message I sent you:

Have you seen the Russian Eurovision entry? The video's great. It's like Ya Ya Europop on *sm:tv*!!

Return the favour then Anthony, read out the last text you sent me.

654, 6trgsjnztt . . . oops, was cleaning my screen.

Clumsy git.

Clumsy git with a clean phone screen, though.

QUESTION 3: What's the most annoying thing about me?

The way you eat a Chinese takeaway.
    Basically, you should NEVER order a Chinese takeaway with Declan Donnelly, because it takes him three hours to finish it.

I like to eat it like I'm in a restaurant.

This is exactly what I'm talking about.

Tell me how you eat a Chinese takeaway then, if you're such an expert.

Like normal people. I get all the dishes out, plonk everything on my plate – a few prawn crackers, couple of spring rolls, some rice, some of my main – then I sit down, eat it and put on a movie.

Madness. Absolute madness. Firstly, you start – and I'm going to shock you here – with the starters, BUT while you're eating them, you keep the lids on all your mains, so they don't get cold.

Haven't you got a 'warming drawer' in your kitchen these days? Cos you're quite well-to-do.

We're getting off the point. I'll pop one chicken satay stick on my plate, where it's joined by one spring roll with a bit

of sweet chilli sauce and a spare rib. I savour them and then it's back to the kitchen to get my first duck pancake. Then I'll have another spring roll.

By this point, I've finished my entire meal. And I'm ready to watch a film.

Then it's time for duck pancake number two, which, crucially, is still nice and warm, as are your mains, which, let's not forget, still have their lids firmly on.

It's now ten o'clock and there's no point in even starting a film . . .

Eventually, after I've finished my meal, with a good pause in between each course, I . . .

You do what? Get the bill? We're not in a restaurant! And I really wanted to watch John Wick 2.
   I just think it says a lot about you.
   It's no wonder you've hardly seen any films. And I bet you don't get to sleep till after midnight, cos you've got to spend an hour on your toothbrush app before you get into bed.
   Your turn.

The most annoying thing about you is your shoes.

What?

Whenever we have to pack a suit and shoes and go somewhere smart, I can guarantee Ant will bring two shoes that don't match.

You make it sound like I've got thousands of pairs of shoes.

That's the thing, you haven't! You just always get them mixed up and bring odd pairs. You've worn odd shoes for a final of *Britain's Got Talent* and we nearly missed the National Television Awards one year cos of your absent-minded footwear folly.

'Footwear folly' – you've been saving that one up, haven't you?

Allow me to elaborate. We were filming *BGT* auditions in Cardiff and were getting a private jet to get back to London for the NTAs.

Think the words 'private jet' may have just lost the readers' sympathy. . .

We get our suits ready to check we've got everything and Ant realises he's got two odd shoes. This results in Joe, our driver, having to hot foot–

Is that a shoe pun?

Yeah, why not?
   Joe has to hot foot it to Chez McPartlin, collect a matching pair of shoes (and frankly, I'm surprised such a thing exists. . .) and meet us at City Airport, so Ant can put on the right shoes for the ceremony.

There's no way this is worse than the way you eat a Chinese.

It's just daft and it leads to fannying about.
   And you know I don't like fannying about.

QUESTION 4: What's the most memorable holiday we've had together?

Easy. Antigua.

Do we have to bring this up?

Yes, we do. It was during our pop star days. We got a week off and we decided to go somewhere hot.

We'd never been to the Caribbean and I was so excited. I'd never even heard of Antigua. But it was so hot. I mean, I'd been hot before, but this was a different kind of hot. Our room had a ceiling fan, but it was right above one of the single beds, a fact Ant noticed before I did.

You bet your life I did. The second we walked into the room, I chucked my bag on the bed underneath it like a shot. If you weren't under that fan, that room was sweltering. Not just a pretty face, eh?

Yeah, yeah, very clever.
　　On the first day, we went out to the beach and I went for a paddle, then headed back to my sunlounger. My feet were covered in sand from the beach and I remember thinking, 'They'll be all right, your feet don't burn, do they?'
　　How wrong I was. That night my feet were so burnt they were bright purple – they were all blistered and swollen. I literally couldn't walk.

I, on the other hand, literally couldn't stop laughing.

I couldn't even put shoes on. I had to sit with them in a bath full of cold water. I ended up staying in the room for four of the seven days we were in Antigua. I lived on room service.

I would go to the buffet at breakfast and bring a plate back to the room for Dec and then, in the evenings, he would sit in the room on his own while I went to the TV area and watched Seinfeld.

I was stuck there with a Sega Game Gear and the door to the balcony open. A couple of times, I saw people walk past the room and heard them say, 'That must be him, the boy with the burnt feet.' All because some loudmouth told everyone in the TV area about my predicament. I wonder who that was . . .

Let's move on, shall we?

Fine. My most memorable holiday was probably when we went to Cala Millor in Spain in 1997, where I got my revenge on you for telling everyone about my burnt bloody feet. There were games played round the pool every day – shuffleboard competitions, dance-offs, relay races – and I signed up Ant for every single one of them without telling him.

The entertainment officer was a bloke called Jorge and, at the start of each day, he would read out the names of the signed-up participants. When I signed Ant up, something got lost in translation and Jorge thought Ant's name was Andre. So every time a game started, Jorge would get on the mic and say, 'And our first player is Andre!' and I would say to Ant, 'Go on Andre!', and he would have to trudge up to the side of the pool and play a load of games.

I was furious.

Revenge is sweet.

And, worst of all, after Jorge had seen how 'keen' I was on each game, he asked me if I wanted to join the cast of his hotel production of Phantom of the Opera. *He was gutted when I turned him down; he couldn't look at me again.*

I think that's one-all on the holiday front.

QUESTION 5: When did I make you laugh the most?

Probably on a charity golf day in Ireland with Alan Shearer, Rob Lee, Kevin Keegan and a load of other Newcastle United legends. Right from the off, there was what is technically known as 'banter' flying all over the shop.

Let me guess, I was really funny, giving as good as I got and getting loads of laughs?

Not exactly.
I was thinking more of the time we arrived late for dinner and everyone sang 'Heigh-Ho!' to you when you walked in. And then when you went to sit down, Shearer had got the waiter to replace your chair with 'a highchair for Mr Donnelly'. I've never laughed so hard in my life.

That's more 'the time you've laughed at me the most', rather than the time I made you laugh the most, isn't it?

To-may-toe, to-mar-toe.

OK, if that's how we're playing it, then the time you 'made me laugh the most' was when we were at the London Studios and they'd just painted the place. Along with various other members of the *Saturday Night Takeaway* **production team, we were walking down the stairs and there were signs everywhere — and I mean everywhere — with 'Wet Paint' written in large and very clear letters.**

There weren't THAT many signs.

There were loads of them.
    The best thing was that I knew exactly what was going to happen the minute I saw those signs. And, sure enough, after taking about three steps down the stairs, Ant reached out with what can only be described as gusto, gripped the bannister and covered his entire palm in fresh green paint.
    It is comfortably the most I have laughed in the 30 years we've spent together. I can still see your green hand now.

Whose idea was this whole five questions thing anyway?

Yours.

Let's just get to the Epilogue, shall we? I'm washing my hands of this.

Just like you did after you grabbed that bannister.

Get a grip.

Just like you did with that bannister.

Epilogue! Now!

- On Wednesdays we wear
animal hats -

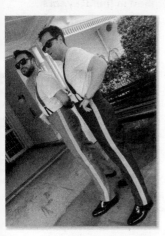

- This is a great angle for us -
must remember for future. -

- Sitting for our Madame
Tussauds' waxworks. -

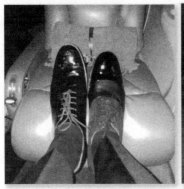

- Case in point: Ant's odd shoes. -

– With our puppies when they were puppies. –

– Our joint 40th birthday part

– Dressed the same. –

– Making sausages in our spare time. –

– The Best Man and the Groom. –

EPILOGUE

Writing this book has been brilliant, emotional, strange, exciting, hilarious and embarrassing all at once. It's taken every emotion, because there's 30 years of two people's lives in these pages.

I'll tell you what we didn't expect, though: to be working on it without being in the same room. A lot of it has been put together during the period of lockdown for Covid-19, and this is the longest Dec and I have gone without being in the same room in the last 30 years. And we've really missed each other.

Too right.

We speak every day, but there's no substitute for being physically with each other. Especially if we're filming anything, either for TV or for social media, normally we're standing side by side, bouncing off each other, making each other laugh — not having that has been very strange. But that's also underlined how incredibly fortunate we are to have each other.

It's also been a process that's made us both take stock of what we've achieved, and the overriding emotions have been an enormous sense of pride and great gratitude.

But I'll tell you what we <u>don't</u> think: 'We've done it.' I don't think we'll ever feel like we've made it — and that's a lot of what drives us.

We're just as motivated as we always have been, if not even more so, to do better work. Part of that is that we've started thinking about our legacy, about what we'll leave behind for people to watch.

In other words, it's time to start thinking about the next 30 years! We still have so much energy and enthusiasm and I sometimes think 30 years won't be enough time; part of me feels like we're just getting started.

Believe it or not, sometimes people ask us for advice, and I guess 'The Gospel According to Ant and Dec' is a pretty simple one. For a start, 'Follow your instincts'. Whenever we've done that, that's when things have worked out best for us. Whether that's quitting our music career, doing *Pop Idol* or getting Alan Shearer to make us a cup of tea. Your gut instincts are the best guide you'll ever have.

And stick together. Trust in each other. And if you ever feel like you don't deserve something, or you wonder why good things are happening to you, then stop.

Because the question you should be asking yourself isn't: 'Why me?'

The question you should be asking is: 'Why not me?'

If we can do it, then so can you.

Grab every opportunity you can and make the most of it. Listen to smart people when they give you advice. And enjoy the ride.

Here endeth the quite quick and simple lesson.

People often ask us what the secret of our success is, and there's a one-word answer to that question: friendship.

It's not much of a secret really, but it's an unbreakable friendship and a deep love for each other. Without that, we've got nothing.

And, crucially, a friendship that right here, right now, has never, ever been stronger.

Right, you're probably sick to the back teeth of us two by now, so to finish 'The Ant and Dec Story' (film rights still available, incidentally), let's hear from a few people you might recognise.

SIMON: 'You don't last this long without being smart. You don't last this long without respecting your audience. They're like brothers.'

DAVID: 'They're going to be on TV for as long as they're both alive and there is TV. They are amazing. There's nobody like them.'

CAT: 'When they come together something incredible happens, something magical. The audience wants to hang out with them and will always invite them into their homes.'

STEPHEN: 'They've got so much warmth. You can't buy that, and you can't learn it. What they're doing is not an act. What you see with Ant and Dec is Ant and Dec.'

ROBBIE: 'What people don't see with Ant and Dec is the hours, days and weeks of complete professionalism and dogged determination to be the very best. They create joy for a living, and I love them both.'

DAVID: 'They're in each other's pockets all the time. You'd think you'd start to get on each other's nerves.'

SIMON: 'They never get bored of each other, which is incredible. It would drive me nuts working with one person the whole time.'

Hang on, those last two make us sound a bit weird. We can't leave it like that.

You're right, we don't live in each other's pockets.

Course not.

Now, no hogging the duvet tonight, OK?

Promise.

THANKS

Thank you to our editor Emily Barrett and the whole team at Little, Brown for allowing us to look back over our 30 years together, it has been a joy working with you.

To Andy Milligan who helped us write it in between discussing the fate of Newcastle United.

To our wonderful management team at YMU Group (formerly James Grant), we could never thank you enough for so much.

To every person we have worked with, behind and in front of the camera. There are so many of you that have played a part in us being at this point in our lives and career and we thank you. There are too many to mention, just as there were too many stories to include in this book, but we are grateful and appreciative of the effect you have had on us and our journey.

To our friends and families, thank you for your continued love and support.

And finally, to all the people who have watched, enjoyed and supported us along the way, it's you who keeps us going and drives us forward. We could never have dreamt back in 1990 that we would be here today looking back over thirty incredibly eventful years and it's thanks to you that we are. We reserve the biggest and most sincere thanks of all to you. We look forward to creating the next chapters of our story together with you.

Here's to the next 30 years!

– Dec's stag do. Ant meets his
childhood idol 'Kevin Keegan'. –

– In Australia. Petting a kangaroo
that looks, at best, indifferent. –

– 'Just put the wigs on and
smile, it's not like anyone'll
ever see this photo.' –

– No one'll recognise us with caps
on . . . just as long as they haven't
got our initials on. Dammit! –

PHOTO CREDITS

Andy Clifford: pages 7 middle, 171 bottom left, 212 bottom, 230 middle left, middle right and bottom right, 235 top right, 245 middle left, 250 middle right

Andy Milligan: pages 180 bottom left, 296

BBC Photo Library: pages 16, 33 top left and right, 37 top

Chloe Brown: pages 75 middle, 97 top

Claire Horton: pages 102 top and middle right, 106 top

Claudine Taylor: pages 245 bottom right, 301

David Walliams: pages 75 top left, 245 middle right and bottom left

Gemma Nightingale: page 303

Greg Barnett: page 89 bottom right

Ian Davison: page 25 top right

ITV: pages 180 top and bottom right

John Jefferson: page 25 bottom right

John Marshall/JMEnternational: pages 112, 120 bottom

Justin Goff/GoffPhotos.com: pages 6 top, 82, 89 top and bottom left, 97 middle left

Kate Mallet: page 75 bottom

Melanie Meakin: page 48 top left

Ollie Green: pages 102 middle left, 106 middle and bottom, 111 top, middle right and bottom

Ian West/PA Archive/PA Images/NTAs 2012 Opening: page 126 middle, Jonathan Brady/PA Archive/PA Images: 221 middle right

Pete Ogden: page 221 middle left

Prince's Trust: page 212 top, middle right

Rachel Jones: page 235 bottom right

RANKIN: page 67 top right

Andre Csillag/Shutterstock: pages 38, 55 top right, 55 bottom, Shutterstock: 41 top left, Action Press/Shutterstock: 41 top right, Tony Ward/Shutterstock: 41 bottom, Edward Hirst/Shutterstock: 55 top left, Greg Williams/Shutterstock: 67 top left, Edwin Walter/ Shutterstock: 67 middle, Iris Honold/Shutterstock: 67 bottom, Ken McKay/Shutterstock: 70, Fremantle Media/REX/Shutterstock: 98, ITV/Shutterstock: 154 bottom, 204, 221 top right

Sinead McKeefry: page 120 middle

Streeter Lecka/Getty Images: page 131 top left and bottom left

Thames/Fremantle: pages 102 bottom, 110 middle left

All other photos from the authors' own collections.

We asked you to share your favourite moments from the last thirty years and we were overwhelmed by the response. Thanks so much to everyone who sent one in.

It was so tricky to pick just ten, but here goes! Thanks for being the best fans. We hope we can make another thirty years of favourite memories for you.

Without doubt it has to be seeing PJ and Duncan perform at Peterborough Truck Fest (I have photos). I made my friends wait for over three hours so we would secure a place at the front. It turned out there wasn't too much competition for the front row as the crowd consisted of truckers and bikers!!

CAROLINE SMITH

The past thirty years has been incredible, but the one memory that will stay with me forever is when Ant and Dec found out after thirty years together that they were cousins on their DNA journey! That is the memory that will forever stay with me. It was so inspirational and just incredible.

CHLOE UDEN

SM:TV: The boys losing it when Ant had to read out the 'me dad pumped in the biscuit tin'. Still makes me laugh my pants off.

MELISSA MILLS

It has to be Ant picking up Gillian McKeith's ankle after she fainted on *I'm A Celebrity Get Me Out of Here*. He obviously had no idea what to do so just picked up her ankle. My favourite thing ever. Still makes me laugh so much just thinking about it.

JULIE SMITH

My favourite Ant and Dec memory has to be when they received their landmark award for being on the telly together for twenty-five years at the National Television Awards. Since becoming a fan of the boys from the *SM:TV* era, it was definitely a 'Proud Mam' moment for me.

GEMMA TOLLERFIELD